The Curvy Road

A Memoir

The Curvy Road

A Memoir

J.R. Matsill

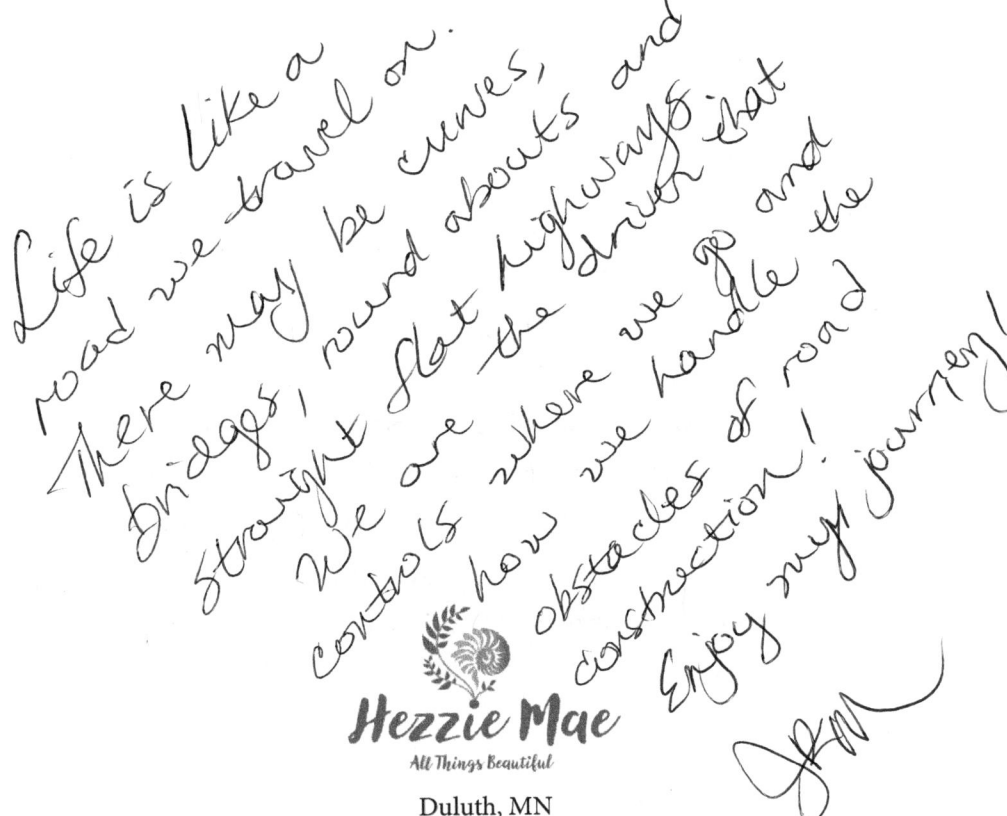

Life is like a road we travel on. There may be curves, bridges, round abouts and straight flat highways that driven. We are the where we go and controls how we handle the obstacles of road construction! Enjoy my journey!

Hezzie Mae
All Things Beautiful

Duluth, MN

Content Warning: This book contains sensitive subject matter pertaining to domestic abuse.

Copyright © 2024 J. R. Matsill

REL Print Group, a Hezzie Mae publication
Duluth, MN
www.HezzieMae.com

All rights reserved. Hezzie Mae supports copyright. Copyright fuels creativity, encourages diverse voices, promotes free speech, and creates a vibrant culture. Thank you for complying with copyright laws by not reproducing, scanning, or distributing any part of this book in any form without permission from the publisher.

ISBN: 979-8-9911532-0-1

I dedicate this book to my wonderful children, their spouses, and my fun-loving grandchildren. I love them all so much, and I am very proud of each one of them. Dedication also goes to a dear friend who was there for me in my time of need and still is there for me.

With this book, I hope to inspire others to follow their dreams and have the strength to pursue them no matter how curvy the road gets.

Photo Credit: Chandra's Older Brother

Table of Contents

Part 1: Twists and Turns 1
CHAPTER 1 2
CHAPTER 2 4
CHAPTER 3 14
CHAPTER 4 19
CHAPTER 5 23

PART 2: Sinuous 25
CHAPTER 6 26
CHAPTER 7 29
CHAPTER 8 38
CHAPTER 9 43
CHAPTER 10 50
CHAPTER 11 59
CHAPTER 12 63

Part 3: The Crooked Road 71
CHAPTER 13 72
CHAPTER 14 74
CHAPTER 15 78
CHAPTER 16 83
CHAPTER 17 86
CHAPTER 18 93
CHAPTER 19 100
CHAPTER 20 105

Part 4: The Freeway **113**
CHAPTER 21 114
CHAPTER 22 120
CHAPTER 23 122

Part 1

Twists and Turns

CHAPTER 1

Chandra had gone to lunch with a friend, and they headed back to a small town where she used to live. Her friend mentioned that he had to check on his other friend's family farmhouse since it was abandoned. He asked if she would mind going there first before he brought her back to his home.

She decided it would be fine, but then she realized the farmhouse he was talking about. Anxiety started filling her body.

Chandra had not been there since that cold, dreary wintery night thirty years ago. Her heart started racing as they drove up the long, straight, narrow driveway. She started feeling queasy remembering the horrible details of that night.

Her friend stopped his pickup and said she should come inside with him to ensure everything was okay. Her hand shook as she reached for the door handle and slowly opened the pickup door. She started walking to the farmhouse door, where he held it open.

They entered the farmhouse and turned on the lights. Looking around, the memories came flooding back. She couldn't believe that some of the same furniture was there that she had bought to try to make this farmhouse seem more like home to her. The same dining room table and hutch. The same plaid couch cushions and brown drapes. The brown wooden rocking chair where she remembered sitting.

The scene from years ago raced through her head as the blood raced through her veins. She started to feel very warm. Her body started to shake, and she felt like she was going to faint.

The nightmare that sent her life down that curvy road was returning.

CHAPTER 2

Thinking back, she felt as if eight lives had existed for her. She had lived in many communities, the first of which was the life of her childhood in a small town. After high school graduation, she moved to a slightly larger town for a few years. Then, she moved to a larger city for a new adventure. Another life took her back to a couple of smaller towns. Although she thought she would settle in the last town for the rest of her life, she was then entering life in a slightly bigger town again. At the present time, she lives in a larger city!

Chandra had met many people in her life and had kept some of them as lifelong friends. She had to think back about which part of her life she was in when she met them. Sometimes, she felt like she had been to the place before and got a sense of déjà vu.

This made her wonder if there had been a life before this, as it seemed very real. Could there be reincarnation?

All in all, she felt her life would be a straight, smooth road. Her first dream was to get married, have children, and live the farm life. Little did she know it would be a "curvy road," just like the road near where she grew up.

Her parents guided her growing up and she had a good relationship with them. Their life was a bit harder growing up than hers. Her father was an only child. His mother had a couple of miscarriages before, so they were very grateful that he survived. Her father weighed a little over two pounds when he was born. He fit into a shoe box, and they placed it in the bottom dresser drawer for his crib with a blanket. Her father graduated high school and was a very quiet man. His parents were farmers, and his father was very intelligent regarding the stock market, where he invested his money wisely, so over the years they were considered wealthy. Chandra's mother had a sister and four brothers. Chandra's mother had to quit high school after eighth grade to go to work for the neighbors to do housekeeping and cooking. The wages were around ten dollars per week.

Chandra remembers her grandparents and the good times they had together. Although the sets of grandparents were different.

Her maternal grandparents lived in a smaller cozy home in a small town and her grandmother was a great cook. Chandra's maternal grandmother made the best sugar cookies and lefse. They also had lots of grandchildren!

Her maternal grandfather was excellent at woodworking and built many things for his grandchildren. He made Chandra a wooden cupboard, which she used to store her toy dishes to play restaurant and her school supplies to play school.

Her paternal grandparents were more sophisticated and with having only one child did not have many things for the grandkids to do when they were visiting. They lived in a larger home in a larger town. Chandra's parents would usually take them to a movie while they visited at their home with them. They also lived right over the hill from the public swimming pool, so if the weather was nice Chandra could go to the pool!

Swimming was Chandra's favorite thing to do whether it was in the area lakes or the pools!

Chandra's childhood was very ordinary, growing up in a small community surrounded by relatives. They were farmers. They were the only farmhouse on a mile road. Half of the road was straight, and the other half was curvy.

Chandra had three older sisters, an older brother, and a younger brother. She became more of a tomboy in the middle of two boys. Although her mother wanted her in the house to help her cook, clean, and bake since the older girls were already out of the house, she would have rather been outside on the tractor.

She loved the outdoors!

Chandra was also very good with small children since she had lots of experience babysitting her nieces and nephews as the youngest sister. Chandra enjoyed the time that she spent with them and had many memories. They were mostly good.

One of Chandra's memories was of taking her two nieces and one nephew fishing in the river. She was sixteen, so her nephew was six, one niece was five, and the other was three years of age.

What was she thinking? They could have fallen in the river!

They had a great time even though she was busy untangling lines from the rocks and trees in the water, ensuring the kids didn't fall into the river, and constantly baiting the hooks. They lasted about an hour at the river, and she was exhausted! Of course, they weren't, but they went home anyway. They did not even catch one fish!

Another memory of babysitting another niece and nephew was when her sister and her husband visited his family lake cabin in the summertime. Chandra was asked to go to the lake to help babysit in the evenings when the adults wanted to go dancing or to dinner. Her brother-in-law's sister was two years younger than her, so they got to swim, water ski, fish, or jet ski during the day, but then at night they were the babysitters. They babysat together many times and have many great memories. It was enjoyable to be at the lake. Chandra loved the lake country! Another one of her dreams was to live on a lake someday.

She thought that being by the water was so magical and hearing the waves crash against the shore was so relaxing. This sound is what she would think of to lull her to sleep on nights that she had trouble falling asleep.

The farmhouse where she grew up was built in the year that she was born. Some people thought they had a huge farmhouse and that her family was wealthy. These days, farming was financially sound, but they were not rich. They raised cattle, pigs, and chickens and had a vegetable garden. They lived off the land as much as they could. Her dad planted corn, beans, oats, and alfalfa.

The whole family helped on the farm with chores, weeding gardens, and mowing lawns. Her younger brother was the family's baby, so her mom would let him watch television most of the time. The farmhouse had three levels. There was an unfinished basement with a pool table, pinball machine, old dressers, and antique school desks that they would use to play school, store, and restaurant.

The children also had a basketball hoop in the next room where they could shoot baskets, but it had a low ceiling, so many light bulbs got broken!

The basement had a kitchen and half bath since the family lived downstairs until the whole house was complete. The main floor had a laundry room, kitchen, dining room, living room, bedroom, den, and full bath. The upstairs consisted of three bedrooms, a full bath, and a storage room. Chandra's uncle was a carpenter who built their house with his partner in their carpentry business. The house had very modern designs with built-in dressers, desks, and window seats in some of the bedrooms.

As they grew up in a small community, they were fortunate to have a lovely home and good family values. It was like the television show *Happy Days*.

After football games, Chandra and her friends would go to the local cafe and play tunes on the small jukebox attached to the wall while having hand-packed burgers and delicious malts put in fancy glass malt glasses with whipped cream on top! Her favorite was a strawberry malt.

Junior High school dances were always fun for Chandra to attend with her friends. The boys would be on one side of the gym and the girls were sitting on the other side of the gym. Once the song started playing on the record player, boys would start crossing over the gym to ask the girls to dance.

Who are they going to ask? Is it going to be her? What if it's a boy that she doesn't like? What do you say then?

She had many good times at these dances, getting to know new friends and hanging out with other great friends.

The holidays were always great being with lots of family and having parties at relatives' houses where the women would be talking and cooking in the kitchen while the men played cards. The cousins would be playing board games or sledding outside.

She made many great memories with her cousins.

Chandra's mother always made the holidays seem like a magical time of year. Christmas was Chandra's favorite holiday with lots of decorations, wonderful treats of Christmas cookies that she would help bake, and the famous in fashion Christmas trees that her mother would buy. The favorite one of hers was the silver fake tree with the rotating color wheel behind it to make it sparkle like the colors of the rainbow. Each Christmas was the famous family photo where the girls all had the same red dresses with white lace, and the boys had the same white shirts, bow ties, and gray cardigan sweaters with black pants.

Chandra's mother would also have someone in the family play Santa Claus. The Santa Claus mask was very scary and made out of paper mâché. Santa did always bring treats but none of the children wanted to go near him!

Chandra remembers getting the Kissy doll one year, Baby First Step another year, and numerous Barbie, Ken and Skipper dolls.

With the snow falling against the moonlit sky, listening to Christmas music while dunking her cut out frosted Christmas cookie in milk, Chandra thought it was like the best time in the world!

Between Christmas and New Years the neighbors would come over with sheets over their heads and different masks to hide their faces as if they were the "Julebukks," which means "Norwegian Christmas Ghosts." Chandra's parents would try to guess who they were and then they had to offer them a beverage of their choice. Once this was done, Chandra's parents had to get disguised and tag along with them to other neighbors' homes. This was a fun tradition, but nowadays they would probably be shot!

This straight, smooth road that she was on was great, but then it became curvy when she was twelve years old.

Chandra's older sister, her husband, and her three children moved 1500 miles away to another state. Chandra's mother was very close to this daughter and had a tough time with this move since this family used to live two miles away from the farm where they grew up. Chandra's sister and her family were moving halfway across the United States!

Chandra was feeling sad, too, since she would miss her nephew and nieces terribly along with her sister and brother-in-law.

This made her mother terribly unhappy about this move. Their mother suffered from depression and had many nervous breakdowns. When she was hospitalized for these, one of her grandmothers would come to stay with them.

Chandra's mother was a perfectionist in cooking, sewing, and house cleaning. With six children, a perfect house was almost impossible to keep up. When her mother became overwhelmed with things in life, the nervous breakdowns would happen. She was prescribed sleeping pills to help her relax. In this day and age there wasn't much knowledge regarding mental health issues.

Chandra's mom went to bed one afternoon to take a nap. She was only in her bedroom for a few minutes before she called out, "Chandra, come in here."

Chandra thought that she might be in trouble. But she did not know why she would be in trouble since she hadn't gone anywhere or done anything.

Chandra entered her bedroom quietly and stood beside her mother's bed. Her mother said, "I just swallowed all of these sleeping pills."

Chandra saw the empty bottle on the nightstand by the bed. She immediately ran to the living room with the empty pill container and said in a panic tone of voice, "Dad, Mom has swallowed all of these!"

Her brothers and her dad rushed into the bedroom and scooped her up. Chandra was holding the door open so they could get her to the car. They all got into the car. Her dad backed out of the garage and started to race down the driveway. He had to speed to get to the hospital because it was over seventeen miles away. He was not used to driving fast.

Chandra teased her dad for usually driving below the speed limit that he might get a ticket for driving too slowly!

On the drive, they were all very nervous. Their mother passed out even though they were all trying to keep her conscious. When they arrived at the hospital their dad ran into the hospital to tell the nurses what happened. The hospital nurses and ER staff came out with a stretcher and raced inside. They got her into a room and immediately started to pump her stomach.

Chandra was in panic mode along with her brothers and her dad. What if her mother didn't survive?

Within an hour, their mother was conscious, and her doctor was telling their father that the prescription for sleeping pills would be taken away from her. She was released from the hospital, and they returned home.

Her mother had no sleeping pills from her doctor. She was used to having something to calm her nerves. She had never drunk alcohol before but she tried it and it seemed to help her. The alcohol she could easily buy herself at the local liquor store or send their father there to pick it up since she did not venture out very much.

The mother that Chandra knew began to fade away into someone that she hardly recognized. Her mother stopped getting up in the morning to make breakfast for them. Chandra made sure that they all ate some cereal and drank some juice before they left for school. Her mother stopped going to church and other community events. She was isolating herself and living in her own little world. Her mother started drinking more and more every day.

Chandra felt like maybe her mother was losing her purpose in life since her children were growing up and making lives of their own.

CHAPTER 3

Chandra was used to staying busy and was very independent. She had a babysitting job in the summer when she was fourteen years old for the neighbor. This neighbor lady was one of few of the farm wives that was employed outside of the home. Most of the wives did not work outside of the home at this time.

Chandra was picked up at 6 a.m. to make breakfast for the farmhand and the husband along with their four children. She also had to make dinner, afternoon lunch, and start supper while watching the four children! The days were very busy with lots of responsibility. But she thought that it was worth it since she earned $27.50 for two weeks!

She was very thrilled to have money of her own. She always walked beans and did chores for her parents, but her pay was food, shelter, and clothing. Having money of her own was great! She started saving it for a rainy day, as they say.

Once school started in the fall Chandra was very involved in school activities such as band, choir, FFA, and cheerleading. She worked as a waitress on the weekends and wasn't home that often. She would rather be gone since her mom started drinking in the morning and didn't make much sense by supper time.

Her parents had set rules for the first three siblings, but by the time the last three hit their teenage years, they were very relaxed and tired of disciplining. All they asked was that they be truthful and tell them where they were going and when they would be home.

Chandra was allowed to date at age sixteen. When she was out on a date, they would bring her home and sit out in the car to chat or maybe share a few kisses. Her dad would flick the yard light off and on, off and on, off and on, which was the signal that she had better get inside since that was enough "necking," as her parents called it.

Chandra had a steady boyfriend that was two years older than her. He lived in a neighboring town. Before he graduated from high school, he wanted to give her a promise ring that they would be together after she graduated high school. She felt that she was too young for this kind of commitment, so she declined. Even though he was friendly and good to her, she wanted to be free and have fun with her friends instead of being tied to one person.

Chandra had saved up enough money and bought her own car when she was sixteen years old for one thousand dollars. It was a two-door 1969 Chevy Impala with a gold body and black vinyl roof. She paid for her own car insurance, gas, oil, and any needed repairs. She put a white-and-black checkered piece of carpet in the back window. She thought she had a pretty cool car to drive lots of her friends around in.

Chandra and her friends went to dances on Friday nights to rock and roll bands, dances to old-time music on Saturday nights with their parents, and on Sunday nights to dance to '50s music.

One Sunday night there was a dance and best dressed '50s costume contest. One of her girlfriends and Chandra dressed in white t-shirts, black scarves around their necks, pink poodle skirts, white bobby socks, and white tennis shoes. They looked pretty sharp dancing to the '50s music!

The band chose them as the winners that night. They won a small cash prize and got to go backstage to meet the band. The band also offered them a beer, but then realized they weren't of drinking age.

Chandra had so many good memories of those dancing days.

The bands they would follow were Shaw Allen Shaw, Jesse Brady, The Happy Wanderers, and Rockin' Hollywoods. A bunch of her friends went to the neighboring town to see Tommy James and the Shondells. She also saw the Charlie Daniels Band when she was in high school. Chandra really liked going to concerts, too!

There wasn't that much to do in the small community where she lived so they had to drive at least thirty miles to go shopping, movies, dances, and concerts.

Many weekends were just getting together uptown and driving the few blocks of the main street. There was a constable in the small town and many guys would play tricks on him. One time they switched the license plates on the vehicles and then raced out of town. The constable would call in the car racing to the county sheriff department and find out it was his car! Good thing these guys never got caught for doing that!

Another time her friends uptown dared Chandra to squeal her tires as she left town. She decided to take them up on that dare. The tires squealed as she burned rubber out of town. She was a mile down the highway when the cop lights started flashing so she pulled over. The constable came up to the driver's window and she knew she was in trouble, but she wanted to laugh.

She was smiling inside since she didn't even know she was able to burn rubber! The constable handed her a ticket for twenty-five dollars. Chandra told him that her friends dared her to do it as she was blinking her eyes and pretending to shed a tear so that he might feel sorry for her. She wiped her tears away and said that she promised that she would not do it again. He then proceeded to tear up the ticket and write one up for a warning. He told her that she was free to drive home.

Chandra let out a sigh of relief. She was glad she didn't have to pay a fine. She liked to spend her money in different ways than that!

There were also keg parties in gravel pits down by the river or at abandoned farms. She just had to be careful at these parties to know where to run if the cops showed up! Sometimes there would be bands playing in a hip roof barn with barn dances. Chandra really enjoyed the barn dances with bales of hay to sit on while listening to great music. It was also really fun to dance on the wooden barn floor.

Neighbors would have dances in their basement and sometimes they invited a local band. The band members were friends, so they used it as practice time. Sometimes there would be dances in the Quonset if it didn't have grain or farm equipment inside. The Quonset was made into a huge dance hall.

Chandra felt as if she didn't have a care in the world since life was about having fun with friends and family!

CHAPTER 4

When her older sister and her family moved, her parents took her and her younger brother on the Amtrak Train to visit them. Chandra's parents didn't travel much, and on the train, they staggered without even drinking! She was sure they were drinking since that was what they did. They had a dome car on the train. Since it was a thirty-six-hour trip, Chandra and her brother roamed the train cars. Chandra was sixteen, and he was fourteen years old.

One night, after supper, she went up to the dome car to sit. A sixteen-year-old boy came and sat with her. He was very nice and pleasant. His dad was the engineer on the train, so he took many trips. He was going to see his brother. They visited until her dad appeared and told her to come to their train car since it was getting late.

They exchanged names and addresses since this was long before email or cell phones. They wrote letters to each other, and he invited her to his prom that spring of 1975. Chandra's mother said that he had to come to their home first before she could visit him. He came to her high school prom in her junior year, and then she took the train to go to his prom. They had a great time! Although, during his visit he thought that the state she lived in was too flat with lots of farmland. He was not used to seeing the horizon since he lived in a valley surrounded by beautiful mountains.

Chandra's older sister, her husband, and three children liked where they lived. Her brother-in-law drove a truck for a company selling frozen food and ice cream products. But then the road got curvy for them when her brother-in-law started having back problems and could no longer drive the truck.

Chandra's mother begged them to move back near them. Her older sister paid for an airline ticket for Chandra to fly out there so she could help her drive their car with three children while her husband drove the U-Haul truck. Chandra asked her older sister if they could make a pit stop to see her guy friend that she had met on the train.

Her older sister agreed to take a break so Chandra could visit with him for a few minutes. He was surprised to see her since this was way before cell phones, so she could not text him to tell him they were stopping by! He had wanted Chandra to move by him after she graduated in May. Chandra considered moving there.

Thoughts went through her mind that she should leave her area and be adventurous. She had other thoughts that she would not be close to her family, and she was unsure about moving out of the state where she grew up.

Her plans to move there fizzled since she was too scared to move that far away. Chandra wanted to go to college to become a Dental Hygienist. This was also scary since only two hundred out of thousands got into the program after one year of taking general education classes. The cost of college was also scary, at approximately $2,500 per year, which she had to pay for herself. At the time, vocational school costs were more reasonable. Weighing all the facts, she decided to attend a vocational school for dental assisting starting in November.

In May, Chandra graduated from high school. She worked for a dentist in a nearby town until she moved to attend vocational school in November. One of Chandra's girlfriends came with her to give her two weeks' notice to the dentist she was working for since she was leaving the area to start school. She went into his office while her girlfriend was waiting in the lobby. He knew she would be leaving since she was going to school, but he started to throw pens and slam down books when she told him this. He said that he would miss his "Little Teddy Bear" and he tried to hug her. She backed away and told him that she would not be back to work for him. Chandra almost ran out of that office! Her girlfriend heard the ruckus and they left frantically!

Chandra wondered what had gotten into this dentist. He was always very nice to her and pleasant to work with but why did he cause such a scene? When had she ever been his Little Teddy Bear? She was very glad to get out of that situation.

This same girlfriend was two years younger than her, and she was having trouble living with her adoptive parents. Chandra was eighteen years old and legal age, so they went to court to see if she could get custody of her. They thought that she could come to live with Chandra, where Chandra would work part-time for a dentist after her classes at the vocational school, and her friend could finish high school.

The judge granted custody of a sixteen-year-old to Chandra, an eighteen-year-old! Chandra thought that this was a crazy curvy road, but she was excited to have her friend move with her. She wouldn't feel so alone moving to a new town!

Together, they were all set to move into the apartment when one of her sisters said it would be a lot of responsibility for Chandra. After thinking it over Chandra decided not to have her friend move with her. Chandra's oldest sister offered to let her live with her family to continue high school and graduate.

CHAPTER 5

Chandra moved into the furnished apartment by herself. Before beginning dental assisting school, she started working at the dental office in that town to earn extra money to pay for gas, groceries, and apartment rent. At age eighteen, she was on her own without any financial help from her parents, which taught her to be even more independent. Because of this, she was a very dependable, responsible person.

Chandra felt very confident. She felt like she would be able to conquer anything at this point in her life.

Chandra was feeling a bit lonely since she did not know anyone in this town that she had just moved to except for the few that worked at the dental office. She would go to work and then just go back to her apartment.

Out of the blue, a classmate from high school called her and asked her to go with him to the Elvis Presley concert. He was a huge Elvis fan and had all of his memorabilia. Chandra enjoyed concerts and liked Elvis' music so she said she would go with him. Chandra also felt like she had something fun to look forward to!

Elvis was not in the best shape at the concert and could not even finish a song. It was disappointing yet very cool when Elvis threw a scarf Chandra's way. She had her hand on the scarf, but a stronger guy behind her grabbed it out of her hand! Chandra should have fought harder for the scarf since it would have been worth lots of money now, but she just let it go with the disappointing show that he put on.

She did get a picture of Elvis since they snuck down to better seats. In this day and age, they didn't have security checking your tickets, so you could quickly move to better seats and pay a lot less money for your ticket! Seeing how close you could get to the stage was always fun. Chandra was glad that she saw Elvis in person since he was the "King of Rock and Roll." He was also known as "Elvis the Pelvis" since he could shake those hips! Elvis Presley died on August 16, 1977. Years later, Chandra visited his home and grave in Graceland, Tennessee.

PART 2

Sinuous

CHAPTER 6

Once school started in November, Chandra met friends also enrolled in the same program. She was living by herself in an upstairs apartment above a theater. A friend from high school was also enrolled in the secretarial program at the vocational school, so they decided to get a bigger apartment and share the expenses in the same building. Chandra went to the vocational classes for dental assisting in the morning and worked at the dental clinic in the afternoon. A female co-worker suggested going to the bar after work one night, so they did.

At that bar, Chandra met a guy who was a farmer. His name was Earl. He had coal-black hair with a full beard. He was husky, weighed about 210 pounds, and was about six feet tall. He lived with his family on the farm and was four years older than her.

A dream of hers was to live on a farm and raise her family just as she had been raised, except to omit the alcoholism.

Earl was a funny guy, but he did like to visit the bars. Once in a while he would call the dental office and would ask to talk to her married female friend to invite her to the bar after work. She then invited Chandra to come along. Chandra thought they were having an affair. She found out later that Earl was just trying to get to know Chandra. Earl and Chandra started to date off and on.

Chandra graduated from dental assisting and had a job offer in another city five hundred miles away. Earl begged her not to leave the area, so she turned down that job and became employed thirty miles away.

A former dental assisting classmate was also going to work in the same neighboring town, so they decided to rent an apartment together. Chandra still continued to date Earl even though he liked to frequent the bars where he lived.

On Chandra's twenty-first birthday, Earl asked Chandra to marry him and gave her an engagement ring. She said, "Yes."

The next day, when she looked in the box the engagement ring came in, Chandra saw that the receipt had a purchase date of 1975.

He didn't even know her then, so she questioned him. He explained that he bought this for a girl who now lives in another state, and she told him no when he popped the question.

This didn't make Chandra feel good. She felt like the ring should be special and purchased specifically for the person it was intended for.

Earl told Chandra that the date he bought the ring shouldn't matter. So, she put her hurt feelings aside and stuffed them away.

They decided to get married in February 1979.

She wore her mother's pure satin wedding dress. It had a long train and buttons. Her mother was going to make all the beautiful silk flowers for the wedding.

During their engagement, Earl would forget to call her for a date, but he would go to the bar with friends. When she questioned him about this, he said it would all change after they got married.

Chandra visited her second oldest sister, who had been married for several years, to ask for advice. She told Chandra that her husband never did this to her and still doesn't treat her like that. Chandra wanted to call off the wedding, but her mother had done so much work, and her father had already paid for the wedding venue, food, and band.

She thought positively that Earl would change for the better after they were married.

CHAPTER 7

When they were married, Earl did not want Chandra to work. She had been working for a paycheck since she was fourteen years old! She wanted to work. Chandra was an extrovert and liked being around people.

How would the bills get paid?

Earl was farming his dad's land, and they lived in the farmhouse where he grew up. He was supposed to buy the farmhouse and land from his dad but needed more money. They raised cattle, pigs, and chickens. They also had a vegetable garden but still needed money to pay the bills. Chandra helped with farming the land and feeding the animals. She finally got to drive a tractor!

Even though Earl did not want her to work outside of the home, Chandra started working for a dentist in town so they would have money to pay the bills. She often came home from work to find that he had just left for the bar.

The house was a mess since his brother, father, and himself always had lunch at the family farm where they lived, but nobody ever cleaned up the dishes. The table was full of dirty dishes, which had to be cleaned up before beginning to cook supper. They also never removed their muddy manure boots, so this was scattered throughout the house and needed cleaning. There were many suppers that he never came home for.

Chandra realized that Earl was probably doing these things to punish her for getting a job, but she loved her work and her coworkers.

This was a curve in the road, so Chandra left and went to her parents' home for the weekend. She never mentioned anything to anyone about her terrible marriage, as she thought it was her problem. The old saying goes, "You've made your bed, now lie in it."

It's an OLD saying!

Chandra had new ways of thinking regarding equal partnership in marriage, but this was totally different from Earl's old-fashioned way of thinking.

Earl called her while she was there and wanted her to come home, promising he would change if they had children. Chandra had always wanted children, but he was reluctant because they would interfere with his freedom and be an added expense.

Chandra was very excited when she became pregnant! She thought that this would be great for their marriage also.

While she was pregnant, Earl was mad that some machinery had broken down, so he came in the house and threw Chandra on the floor then stomped out of the house and slammed the door. He got in his pickup and went to the bar.

Chandra got up off the floor teary eyed and feeling so sad. She was scared that having the baby was probably not going to change things in her marriage.

She had a son in August of 1981 after being induced for eight hours since the baby was ten days overdue. He was born a cute, healthy, wonderful boy! Earl went to the bar every night for weeks after their son was born. He said that he was celebrating.

Chandra felt very alone even though she had many visitors coming to see her and their baby boy in the evenings. She thought that Earl should be there with them. She wondered what her visitors thought when Earl wasn't home so she would tell them he was busy in the field. Why was she lying for him?

Chandra had started working part-time at the bank before her son was born, so life was good, except for her relationship with her husband. Their relationship could have been better. A lot better!

If he did not get in a fight at the bar, he would instigate one with Chandra when he got home. Earl told Chandra that her clothes and hair were ugly. He also said that she didn't know how to cook, clean, or do anything right. He would slap her hard on her cheek.

Tears would well up in Chandra's eyes, but she was afraid to cry since he might strike her again.

The next day after work Chandra picked up her son at daycare and drove to the women's shelter because she feared Earl's temper and was very nervous around him. The women's shelter advocates were very helpful with information and Chandra was glad that she came. She explained to them that she tried to do everything perfectly so as not to make Earl angry, but he was still physically and verbally abusive to her. They told her that it was not her fault and that nobody should be treated that way.

Chandra felt much better but knew she had to go back to try to save her marriage and hoped that Earl would change.

Earl did not change. He kept getting into trouble with DUIs and bar fights, where the local police had to intervene because they knew his temper.

Earl was sentenced to Project Turnabout after a second DUI, and Chandra had to attend the family group sessions. Chandra would have her mother-in-law watch their son. In the last session Earl attended, he threw a folding chair across the room full of thirty people! Everyone gasped and moved quickly to avoid having the chair hit them. Then Earl stomped out of that treatment center. The counselors told Chandra that she was dealing with a ticking time bomb and would never know when Earl would explode again. Earl said that he would change after having a child. He did not.

On August 13, 1983, Earl came home drunk at 1:30 a.m. and said that the neighbor had given him a ride home. He then passed out in the bed.

The phone rang at 4 a.m., and it was Chandra's older brother who was sobbing, telling her that her oldest sister, who had moved back to their hometown, had died in a car accident. Chandra went to the bedroom and shook Earl's shoulder to wake her drunken husband. She then picked up her sleeping almost two-year-old son and headed for the car to get to her brother-in-law and his three children. Earl staggered to the car and got in the passenger side.

Earl was passed out while Chandra drove. Her son stayed asleep the whole time too. Chandra was in shock and didn't know how they even got to her parents' home in the neighboring town. Chandra wasn't thinking since she should have driven to her sister's home. It was her niece's twelfth birthday, and her niece's mother (Chandra's older sister) had just died!

Chandra was trying to keep it together without being hysterical, but this was such terrible news.

Her parents were not there, but a higher power must have told her to travel in that direction because she had seen her other sister's black van in the driveway of her sister's mother-in-law's house. She pulled up in their driveway and knocked on the back door. Her sister's mother-in-law answered the door at 6 a.m., wondering why Chandra was in such a panic.

Chandra asked, "Where is my sister?"

Her sister's mother-in-law answered, "They are sleeping in the basement bedroom." Chandra ran down the stairs quickly and found her sister sleeping. Chandra shook her shoulder until she woke up. She was startled to see Chandra standing at her bedside, especially at that time of the day.

Chandra told her that their oldest sister had been killed in a car accident, and they needed to go to her house. She said she would get dressed, wake her husband and son, and they would soon be there.

They had been on vacation in Sturgis, South Dakota, so they weren't able to be reached. Again, there were no cell phones at this time.

Chandra was just glad that she had mistakenly gone the wrong direction. Chandra, Earl, and their son arrived at her sister's home, where her parents and the other siblings were helping her brother-in-law, who was hyperventilating due to the tragedy. Chandra's nieces and nephews were crying upstairs in their bedrooms.

Chandra brought her son upstairs to talk with her nieces and nephew. They were all crying, and in the midst of it all, massive tears started rolling down Chandra's cheeks. Chandra's son looked at her very confused but gave her a smile and a big hug. Her nieces and nephew did not want to talk about anything, so she left them alone to go downstairs and join the rest of the family.

Everyone was in shock. Chandra's brother, who had called about her sister's death, started telling the story of what had happened. Chandra's niece was camping with many friends in her sister's backyard for her twelfth birthday. Chandra's brother was going through a divorce then, and their sister went out to visit him since he was confused about life. He did not realize that his oldest sister had been drinking, or he would have never wanted her to be driving to his house (the family farm) three miles from her home. She took the gravel road out to the house to avoid any cops. Apparently, she swerved for something in the road, lost control, and rolled the car. She was not wearing a seat belt (back then, there was no seat belt law), so she flew from the vehicle, and the car landed on top of her. After a while, one of the neighbors was driving home on that road and saw the car. He called the authorities, who notified Chandra's older brother. Chandra's oldest sister was the mother of a fifteen-year-old son, a fourteen-year-old daughter, and a twelve-year-old daughter. It was a very tragic day for all of her family.

Funeral services were made. Her brother-in-law stated that his wife never wanted an open casket. Since the car had landed on top of her it was best that it was a closed casket. So, the funeral for Chandra's sister was a closed casket. With the sudden shock and not seeing her lifeless body, it did not seem real.

Her children had a tough time accepting the fact that their mother was gone. Having an open casket would have given closure to the family. They always thought she was out just getting groceries and would soon walk through the door.

It was hard for any of the family to accept the fact that she had died. Chandra's mother was devastated by the loss of her oldest child.

Even though there was much sadness for Chandra's mother, Chandra and her other sister were both pregnant at the time of their sister's funeral, but they had not told anyone. So, together, they tried to bring some good news to the family.

Chandra was due to have her baby in the middle of January, and her sister was due in the middle of February. This brought some happiness to their mother, but she was still very sad since she was very close to her oldest daughter.

Chandra thought that losing a child would be a terrible thing in life, so she couldn't even imagine what her mother was going through.

Chandra's mother became very depressed. She began to drink more and more every day. Chandra's older brother and younger brother were still living with her parents. Her older brother was farming with her dad while her younger brother was working in a factory in a small town.

One night, Chandra's younger brother went to the bar, drank too much, and received his third DUI. Chandra's mother called her the next day.

Chandra's mother said, "Your younger brother is in jail due to his third DUI."

Chandra replied, "Maybe all this drinking needs to stop!"

Chandra had a husband, mother, and brother who were still drinking and getting into trouble after her sister was killed while drunk driving. Chandra did not dislike drinking until it started to cause family problems.

Her reasoning was that drinking was okay in moderation and for having fun! Drinking was also a good way to relax. Drinking was not fun when it started to make life a curvy and dangerous road!

CHAPTER 8

Earl had quit drinking in November 1983, but he was a dry drunk and still abusive. He would throw things, slam doors, and swear when things didn't go his way. Chandra left him to get her own apartment with her son when she was eight months pregnant due to the abuse. Earl promised her he would change again and wanted her back before the baby was born. Chandra moved back with him to the farmhouse since she did really want this marriage to work. She wanted a husband and children and to have the farm life she had grown up with.

This was her first dream, and she hated to give it up, except sometimes it was a nightmare living with a controlling, abusive husband.

In January 1984, on a Friday night, Chandra came home from work with her son. Earl ate supper with them, and as Chandra was putting the dishes in the dishwasher, she had a very bad labor pain that made her unable to stand up.

Chandra gasped, "I think it is time to go to the hospital."

They drove ten miles to the hospital. Earl dropped her off and then went with his son to his parents' house, expecting it to take eight hours of labor again. The nurse brought her to a hospital room. She gave Chandra a gown and told her to undress and put the gown on. She left the room. Chandra was still having trouble standing up straight due to the excruciating labor pain, but the nurse came back and brought her to the delivery room.

She still had her knee socks on when they pulled up her gown! The doctor and nurse laughed, but they understood why she couldn't remove her socks. The baby was on the way forty-five minutes after her first labor pain! The nursing staff quickly called Earl to get him back to the hospital. He couldn't believe how quickly the delivery was happening. They were blessed with a beautiful healthy baby girl.

Their daughter loved to be put down for her naptime by lying on her stomach with her buttocks in the air while sucking her thumb. She was a perfect baby also. However, their two-and-a-half-year-old son wanted his mom to bring the baby girl back to the hospital. He liked being an only child and was a bit jealous.

Even though Earl was abusive and still struggled with alcoholism at the time, Chandra still wanted another child, as she wanted their son to have at least one sibling. Earl said that he would change after they had children. He did not. He started drinking again.

Chandra felt that other people were wondering why she wanted another child. She thought that they were putting her down since they knew she had moved out on Earl, and she was not feeling much support while pregnant with their second child. But Chandra kept her head held high in the community because she loved being a mom and loved her children. She did not care what others were saying.

Chandra went back to working at the bank in town after eight weeks of paid maternity leave. One day, the deputy sheriff came in to talk with her privately. Chandra asked to use the manager's office. They were granted permission, entered the office, and closed the door. Deputy Codingham was very husky, 6'2", weighed at least 250 pounds, and had reddish hair.

Deputy Codingham said, "With Earl drinking again in the bars so often getting into fights, I am worried about your safety and your children's safety. I could easily pick him up for another DUI, but that might cause more trouble for you. I want you and your family to be safe."

Chandra told him, "I have been at the women's shelter, but I returned to Earl since I want this marriage to work. He keeps telling me that he will change. I am hoping that he does. Also, divorce is not common these days. I will be careful and will notify you if I need you. I will start reporting to you any more abuse I suffer."

Chandra had never reported any of the physical abuse that she had suffered before to the law enforcement. She thought that it was her problem to deal with and things would get better with Earl. Chandra had even come into work a few times with bruises on her arms and even a black eye. She made up stories that she was clumsy and bumped into things. Never in her life did she ever think that she would put up with this!

Thinking back to high school, Chandra never took any grief from anyone. She broke up with boyfriends if they stood her up or were mean to her. She was not afraid to be alone so why was she putting up with this now and not saying anything? Why was she lying about things?

Chandra was afraid of Earl and nervous each day after leaving work about what might happen that evening. Earl would go to the bar before she got home with the children after work and not return until after the bar closed. This was what made her nervous.

What would he do when he came home? Would he pass out, or would he start fighting with her and hit her?

A few times after work, as she drove up the long narrow driveway with the children in their car seats, the cattle were walking down the road to meet them. The cattle had broken the fence since they were hungry.

Chandra put the car in park, turned it off, and opened the door. She ran with her high heels, pantyhose, and dress from work to open the gate and jump into the trailer full of corn to turn on the silage unloader. The forty head of cattle turned around and came one by one through the open gate to start eating the silage as Chandra was scooping corn on top of it.

She then closed the gate and went back to the car to park it close to the house. She got the children out of the car and went into the house with them. Chandra then called the next-door neighbor to come over to help her fix the fence. She had no clue when Earl would be home, and she knew that he would be angry about a broken fence.

There were many times that Chandra relied on the next-door neighbor to help her. It was easier to get a hold of the neighbor than it was to find out what bar Earl was frequenting! Chandra had no clue what the neighbor thought, but she was just grateful that he was helpful.

CHAPTER 9

It was deer hunting season again and many of Earl's relatives would come to stay at their farmhouse. Chandra had made plans with her sister to go to a hotel for the weekend with their children.

Chandra was very happy to be getting away from the farm and the deer hunters for a few days.

On the Friday before they left for the hotel, Chandra's brother-in-law brought her parents to the doctor for checkups since they were not in good health. They were not taking care of themselves properly since her sister died the year before. The doctor found that Chandra's mother had pneumonia, and her father had a blood clot. Chandra's brother-in-law called all the siblings to tell them that their parents were both hospitalized.

Chandra and her sister still went with their children to the hotel and had a great time. They thought that they would be able to visit their parents the following weekend. They didn't think that it was too serious that their parents were in the hospital.

On Monday, November 12, 1984, Chandra was at work and received a call from her older brother that their mother was probably not going to make it, so she needed to get to the hospital right away. Chandra was shocked. She hadn't realized her mother's situation was so serious.

Chandra worked at a bank in town then, so it would take her forty-five minutes to get to the hospital where they were. She quickly gathered her items and called her mother-in-law to see if she was able to pick up her children from daycare and keep them overnight if needed. Chandra knew that it would be impossible to track down Earl. She also didn't trust him to pick up the children from daycare. Who knew where he would be that evening.

Chandra drove as quickly as she could. Her mind was racing once again and she was praying that her mother would be okay. She parked the car in the hospital parking lot and entered the hospital with nervous vibes running through her body.

Everyone else was already there when Chandra arrived at the hospital. She went in to see her mother. Chandra's mother looked like a space alien. She was all bloated. Chandra hardly recognized her. Chandra took her mother's hand and told her that she loved her. She squeezed Chandra's hand, so she knew she had heard her.

Chandra left her room to return to her siblings. The doctor came in to see all of them. The doctor stated that all of her organs were not working properly, and life support was keeping her alive. As for the children, he stated that a decision had to be made to keep her on life support or let her go. Everyone stared at each other in a state of shock. Everyone was silent.

How do you just let your mother die? She was the one who gave them life, made sure they had a good life, and was there for them most of the time.

After a few moments, the doctor returned and told everyone that there was no decision to be made. Their mother had passed on her own.

Chandra's mother had waited for all of her children to get there to say goodbye so she could pass in peace. Tears started streaming down everyone's cheeks. Everyone started hugging each other. Sorrow filled the room.

It was not fun driving on this curvy road.

The siblings all went together to visit their father, who was in another hospital room. As they walked into the room, he said, "Mama is gone, isn't she?"

All of them nodded yes.

They all visited with their dad, and he was very sad. They had done everything together, so he would miss her a lot. He was going to be very lonely.

The doctor told everyone that they would also have to look into a nursing home for their dad since he would not be able to take care of himself. He also, by doctor's orders, was not allowed to go to the funeral since the blood clot in his leg could move and kill him.

Funeral arrangements were held for their mom on November 15, 1984. This date was coincidental since November 15th was their mom and dad's wedding anniversary.

Relatives from all around came. One year and three months after Chandra's sister's death, her mother died. After a few days, the siblings gathered at the family farm to send out thank-you notes. Chandra's children and husband came to the funeral with her. They had driven separately. Chandra was able to stay with her siblings to help write thank-you notes.

All of the siblings then went to visit their dad in the hospital on Saturday, November 17, 1984. He was doing well. He asked how the funeral went and wished he could have been there.

After a few hours, Chandra told him that she was heading home and would come to see him next weekend. After hugging him, Chandra left to return home.

When she got home for the first time after Earl's relatives had been there, she found the house was messy. There were dishes all over, the floor was dirty, and the laundry was piled high.

Nobody was home and it was 5 p.m. Chandra called her mother-in-law to see where her children were. She said she had babysat them for the last couple of days since their dad was busy. Chandra said she would be in to pick them up in a little while since she needed to pick up the house first.

She picked up the children, and shortly after that, Earl returned home after working late in the field.

The following day, Sunday, November 18th, Chandra's sister called her to tell her that their dad had passed away during the night. The doctor stated that the blood clot had moved. Everyone could not decide between two caskets when their mom died, so they decided to choose the other one for their dad. They died six days apart.

Another funeral, different day, same relatives. Déjà vu.

Chandra felt like she was floating in a nightmare that repeated itself.

They say that bad things happen in three ... Chandra's sister's death, her mother's death, and then her father's death.

Now, please let it end!

She wanted to get on the straight road where the driving was smooth! This curvy road was getting out of control!

Earl and their children attended each of the funerals with Chandra. At the cemetery, they were all sobbing. Earl stood back as Chandra's other brothers-in-law hugged and consoled her sisters.

Other friends of the family were holding their children while Chandra and her siblings were grieving. Chandra felt so alone since nobody was holding her as she sobbed. Why didn't she have a spouse who was loving and sympathetic? Instead, she had a spouse that didn't even want to be near her. What had she done to deserve such treatment? She realized that Earl would have more control over her now that her parents were gone. They lived close to Earl's family. Chandra would always visit her parents once a month on the weekends when they were alive since they lived forty-five minutes away. Earl didn't like to go there, so he didn't. Chandra's other siblings also lived at least an hour away.

Chandra felt very lonely even though she was surrounded by family and friends at this time.

Every Sunday after church, they would go to Earl's parents' house for a large Sunday dinner. Earl would act like the perfect husband and father when he was in church, with his family, or at any other public event. Sundays were a bit calmer since liquor stores and bars were closed. Earl did not drink at home. Chandra didn't feel like she was walking on eggshells on this day of the week. She was a bit more at ease on the day of rest.

She wanted to do things for herself and not be imprisoned by her husband even though she knew there might be consequences.

Chandra wanted to join the Jaycee Women in her town so she could meet other women in the community. Earl did not like this, and he said that he would not be watching the children for her to attend these meetings. Earl was still going to the bar nightly.

Chandra was afraid but she wanted to take a chance to join the Jaycee Women. She called the neighbor girl to babysit, and she joined the Jaycee Women and the children had a great time with the neighbor girl. She was always home before Earl came home from the bar anyway, so he didn't even notice she was gone.

Chandra waited a few months to tell him that she was going to these monthly meetings since she knew that he would be very angry.

Chandra finally said one night after dinner, "I have the neighbor girl watching the children once a month while I attend the Jaycee Women's Meetings."

Earl glared at her and shouted, "You should be home all the time and not be running to work or anywhere else! You need to stay home!"

Earl got out of his chair, slammed the door to the house and left in his pickup to go to the bar.

Chandra was shaking with fear but glad that he had left without striking her. What should she do now? Should she go somewhere safe for the night since he might come home and hurt her? She had to work in the morning. The thought of packing up the children's items, finding a safe place to stay and making it to work sounded exhausting. She decided to stay and hoped that nothing would happen when he returned home.

CHAPTER 10

On January 13, 1985, Chandra came home from work with the children at around 5:30 p.m. and nobody was home. They ate supper, but no husband or father was present. She put the children to bed at 8 p.m.

At 10 p.m. Chandra called one of her sisters. Chandra told her sister that she was scared of what Earl might do when he came home.

Her intuition told her that Earl was at the bar drinking.

The counselors at Project Turnabout had stated that he was a ticking time bomb, not knowing when he would explode again. Chandra was very nervous but needed to get to bed since she had to work in the morning.

It was hard for her to fall asleep, so she thought of the soothing sound of the waves hitting the shore of the beach. She was able to fall asleep. Earl came home at 1:15 a.m. and woke Chandra up, threw her out of bed, and slammed the back of her head into the wall.

He then woke up both their children.

Their son was three and a half years old, and their daughter would be one year old soon. Their son started to cry.

Earl was outrageous, screaming and yelling. Chandra grabbed the telephone attached to the wall to call the sheriff.

There was no 911 then, so she had to dial the whole number.

Earl ran to the phone and pushed Chandra out of the way. He then ripped the phone from the wall.

He went to get his shotgun, and he was trying to load it with bullets while shouting, "Nobody else is going to have any of you! If I can't have you, nobody else will either!" He had lost it. Chandra knew that she needed to get help.

How was she going to get help? There was no phone. She couldn't scream for help as the neighbors were too far away.

Earl kept dropping the bullets on the floor. He was so intoxicated he could not get the bullets loaded into the gun. Chandra knew the car keys were in the car, so she had to take a chance to get to the car for help to save them.

It was twenty below zero, and she wore a knee-length flannel shirt for pajamas. She ran out the door barefoot. The ground was freezing cold on her feet, and the air was very chilly. She got to the car. The car started easily, and she put it in reverse to back up and turn around to start going down the driveway. She was leaving her children behind because she thought he would stay there with them. She prayed that he would not hurt them, but she knew she needed to get help!

Chandra drove down the straight, long, narrow, icy driveway and onto the township road. She was shaking with fear. Then, all of a sudden, there were lights behind her! It was Earl in his pickup! He had left the children in the house alone and was following her. Chandra started shaking but she knew she had to keep driving. She reached the highway and turned quickly toward her girlfriend's house, a mile away. She reached her home, and Earl pulled into the driveway behind Chandra's car, so she was trapped.

Chandra ran into her home since the door was unlocked.

She screamed, "Help! Please call the Sheriff!"

This woke up her girlfriend and her husband. It was 2 a.m. and Chandra's scream startled them. Earl shouted out that if they called the sheriff, her husband and her would also be dead since he said that he was definitely going to kill Chandra!

He dragged Chandra to the car, opened the driver's door, and threw her inside, telling her to go straight home. Earl got into his pickup and backed out of the driveway, waiting for Chandra to back out so he could follow her home.

All of this time, she was praying that the children were okay.

When she reached the farmhouse, she ran into the house, and her son was crying. Chandra's daughter was too young to realize what was going on, so she was okay. She was so glad that they were safe!

She picked up both children and got the baby bottle out of the refrigerator. With wobbly legs and shaking hands she moved carefully to the wooden rocking chair. While sitting in the rocking chair, Chandra held both children tightly in her arms. They had their warm footie pajamas on and her daughter was holding her baby bottle. She did not know what to do, so she prayed silently that her girlfriend would call the sheriff, and someone would come to help them.

What could she do? How was this going to end?

She was so scared but knew she had to remain calm and quiet so as not to make Earl any angrier. Earl stood in front of the picture window, trying to load his shotgun. Chandra kept silently praying for help. Time was passing, and she was starting to lose hope that anyone would come to help them.

All of a sudden, she saw headlights coming up the long, straight, narrow driveway. Two people exited the sheriff's car. It was Deputy Codingham (the one who had come to the bank to talk to her) and his partner.

Deputy Codingham had the bullhorn and said, "Earl, put the gun down."

Earl yelled back, "I am going to kill you too, Codingham!"

Deputy Codingham shouted, "Chandra, if you can get out. Get out!"

Chandra realized that she was close to the front door, but it was hardly used so she wasn't even sure if she could get it open.

She had to try to get out! She had to bolt fast and open that door quickly! She also had to hang onto both children as she did this! She said a silent prayer to get them to safety!

Chandra grabbed both children in their one-piece warm footie pajamas and the baby's bottle and ran out the front door.

Chandra left with the clothes on her back, holding the two most precious human beings in her world!

When she reached the sheriff's car, they quickly got them into the back seat and told them to get down. They both had their guns pointed at Earl, and if he had taken a shot, they were ready to shoot him.

He still did not have the bullets in the gun! Thank God for slow, inaccurate responses when drunk!

Deputy Codingham and his partner got into the car and sped down the driveway. They wanted to get Chandra and her children to safety quickly. The deputy sheriff and his partner wanted to take them to a different women's shelter than they had been at before since Earl might follow them there. The women's shelter advocates who knew Chandra's story from being there before wanted her to come there since they already knew her history.

That evening, when this happened, Chandra's girlfriend and her husband, who Earl threatened, did not call the sheriff. She called the women's shelter since she had just been at a Women's Jaycee Meeting with Chandra, and they had speakers from the women's shelter present. She took a pamphlet from that meeting with their phone number. The women's shelter advocate who knew Chandra and her history then called the sheriff's department. Chandra's friend did not know that Chandra had been at the women's shelter. Chandra had told no friends or relatives about the abuse that she suffered from Earl.

They arrived at the shelter shaken from the devastation of the evening. Chandra was exhausted, and her children were frightened. They were taken to a room with a couple of beds.

Chandra put the children in a double bed with her so they could all snuggle together for comfort. After tossing and turning, trying to shake the night's events, sleep overwhelmed all three of them, and they slept into the wee hours of the morning.

There were four other women with children at the shelter. They were all served a delicious, warm family-style breakfast, with everyone in attendance. Everyone introduced themselves and their children. The women's advocates were very friendly and empathetic. There was a sign-up sheet on the wall of the women's duties. They told Chandra not to worry about signing up until she felt like she belonged there. They told her to take care of her children and herself first. The women's shelter had no television or radio, so they could not hear the local news.

Chandra's daughter celebrated her first birthday at the women's shelter. Her daughter did get a couple of small presents from the women's shelter advocates and a small birthday cake.

Chandra felt very sad that her daughter couldn't have a birthday party with relatives and friends gathered around. Chandra felt bad that she wasn't able to give her daughter any gifts, but she felt very grateful that they were in a safe place and alive.

Chandra had family members tell her that they had heard on the radio that Earl had been apprehended and was put in jail the next day after this incident. Bail was set for him at $100,000 for threatening the lives of his wife, children, the deputy sheriff, and her friends. Only 10 percent had to be posted for bail.

Chandra was very exhausted and slept whenever the children took a nap. Chandra also put them to bed at 8 p.m. every night, and she was supposed to come downstairs to attend group counseling sessions but would fall asleep with her children instead. The advocates were worried that she was going through some depression. It had only been two months since she had buried both parents! Now Chandra had her life, her children's lives, her friends' lives, and the deputy sheriff's life threatened.

There was a lot more to deal with . . . the black cloud needed to float away! Chandra was very exhausted! She thought there were way too many curves on this road of her life!

She was granted permission by the courts to take the car from the farm. So, one day one of the women's shelter advocates gave her a ride to the farm to get her car. Chandra's children stayed at the women's shelter with the other advocates. Chandra and the advocate returned to the women's shelter and then they heard the news that Earl had been bailed out of jail. Chandra was so glad that they had not crossed paths with him while they were getting the car!

A few weeks passed, and Chandra and her children still lived at the women's shelter. The advocates at the shelter helped Chandra sign up for several government programs. These included Aid For Dependent Children (AFDC), Medical Assistance (MA), Women, Infants and Children (WIC), and food stamps. Chandra was feeling better, getting her strength back, and feeling more confident. She did not receive money from Earl as he didn't have any. Chandra had been able to save up three hundred dollars in a savings account but that was all the money she had.

After a month, she moved to a low-income apartment building where other single mothers lived, and they had a great support group. Her siblings brought a farm truck to help load up half of the household belongings from Earl's farmhouse.

The sheriff's department had to have one officer there, and they had only one hour to move items out of the house. They worked fast and furious but left a lot behind. Chandra had to have an unlisted phone number and not give out her address since Earl had been bailed out of jail and could still try to hurt them.

Chandra had gone to court to get an order for protection with an advocate of the women's shelter. Chandra, the women's shelter advocate, Earl, and half of his family members were in the courtroom.

Earl's family members had been contacting Chandra's family members and threatening them that if Chandra did not go back to Earl, they were going to pursue taking her son and daughter away from her by proving mental instability.

Chandra should have been crazy for the verbal and physical abuse she had suffered from her husband for six years! But Chandra was a very strong and independent person. She had strength from a higher power that helped her no matter what tall obstacles she may have to climb, pulled her up when she fell into a deep dark hole, and helped her brush off the terrible memories so only the wonderful memories blossomed.

The judge pointed his finger at all of Earl's family members and stated, "If any of you contact Chandra's relatives again, I will put each of you in jail!"

She was very happy to hear this but kept a straight, somber face. Chandra liked that judge!

So, with the order for protection in place, she could feel a little at ease, but the police told her that they may not get there in time, so someone still could get hurt. They told Chandra that she still needed to be very cautious.

CHAPTER 11

A few weeks later, the prosecuting attorney called Chandra and told her that it would be better if a plea bargain was reached so Earl would not get such a lengthy jail sentence. This way, he would be able to keep the family farm and there was less chance of him coming after them to harm them. The prosecuting attorney also suggested that Chandra move far away from the town that Earl lived by but stay in the state; otherwise, he would get three months of custody of their children in the summer.

Chandra agreed to the plea bargain. This would be better for the witnesses involved also since they would not have to testify. Earl had pleaded guilty to kidnapping, false imprisonment, terroristic threats, and assault in the second degree on February 10, 1985. He was sentenced to one year in jail with the Huber Law and five years' probation. Chandra's divorce was final in April 1985. Chandra signed a quitclaim deed, so she was no longer responsible for the farm.

A few months went by, and her ex-husband remained on the Huber Law, where he could get out of jail to work but had to return to the prison by 7 p.m. each night. He did get to see the children once a week on Wednesdays for two hours with supervision from 5 p.m. to 7 p.m., which was strange since he had endangered their lives, but it was court-ordered, so Chandra was told that she would be in contempt of court if she did not comply and she could end up in jail!

Laws sometimes did not make sense to her. Who did they protect?

He had to pick up and drop off the children at a public place and have a relative with him. Chandra chose the women's shelter to be that place since she felt protected there. One Wednesday, Earl came by the women's shelter to drop off the children, but he was holding on to both of them and would not let them go. Earl had their four-year-old son by the arm and was holding their eighteen-month-old daughter. Their four-year-old son was able to get free and ran to Chandra sobbing. Earl threatened to keep their eighteen-month-old baby daughter, so Chandra went to the telephone.

With her trembling hand she dialed the number for the sheriff's department, asking them if Earl did not have to be in jail by 7 p.m. because now the time was 7:15 p.m. They said that he should have returned, and he was in violation. Chandra told the sheriff's department that he was at the women's shelter and threatening to take their daughter away. They sent a squad car over immediately and picked up Earl. He was then sentenced to no visitation for three months.

The bank where Chandra worked had a branch in a city 146 miles away that was going to be hiring a bank teller. She applied and became employed there in June of 1985. Chandra and her children moved into a split lower-level duplex. A single mother with two daughters, ages eight and four, occupied the upper-level duplex. Chandra's siblings once again used the farm truck to haul their belongings. They unloaded items by taking off the ground-level windows and putting them through this opening.

Chandra was very thankful for her siblings who helped her move again! But after her siblings left, Chandra was petrified since she knew nobody, and it was a bigger city than she had ever lived in!

Chandra had not even physically met the daycare provider she would be leaving her children with the next day when she went to her first day of work. So, the children and Chandra drove to the daycare provider's house on Sunday afternoon, but she was not home. Across the street was a park, so they went to play. Chandra sat on the swing with her daughter. Tears of fear ran down her cheeks while her son played in the sandbox.

She felt scared and anxious, not knowing what to expect from this city, her new job, and the new daycare provider.

Chandra was so grateful to have her children, so she wasn't alone. She felt a higher power was there for everyone, so she was never really alone. Her faith in a higher power had helped her through many struggles in life.

Chandra felt that if you believe, then anything is possible!

Chandra went to drop off her children at daycare, and the provider was very nice. Chandra was on a sliding fee daycare through the county, which helped since she only made twelve dollars an hour at the bank. She did get health insurance benefits for herself, but the children were on medical assistance. She was supposed to receive $275 in child support but sometimes never saw this money from her ex-husband, or he was months behind. There was a great child support collector system in the county where she lived so they were very helpful in sending certified letters to Earl when he was in arrears. Earl thought that Chandra was spending the child support money on going out to the bars and having fun. That was the last thing on Chandra's mind to be spending money on! She needed it to support her children with food and clothes!

Wow! The crazy way some people think!

She walked into the bank and met the eight people she would be working with. They were all very nice. This was starting to feel comfortable. Chandra and her children's home was cozy, and they all made terrific adjustments. Her four-year-old son would play with the four-year-old girl from upstairs. These two would also throw cut grass at the guy who mowed the lawn while Chandra and her daughter were inside laughing. The lawnmower guy always cut the grass with his shirt off and was sweaty, so the blades of green grass stuck to his hairy chest. As they threw the grass, he just kept mowing the lawn, never saying a word. Chandra thought this was hilarious!

CHAPTER 12

An old boyfriend had asked Chandra to take a motorcycle trip to Sturgis. Since she was a single mom, her ex-husband was still in jail, and with no reprieve for her, she checked with the neighbors to see if they could watch her two children. The neighbors to the left were a wonderful couple with children ages seventeen, fifteen, and thirteen that would babysit for the week while Chandra was on the trip.

She had never gone on a long motorcycle trip, especially to the wild and crazy Sturgis Rally, but her sister said she would have a blast!

As the group of ten bikes departed from a small town near her hometown, she thought, *What am I doing? What if I get killed and have two orphaned children!* She then said a quick prayer that all would be safe on the ride, and she let her long, black hair blow in the wind.

Her troubles also blew away in that wind . . . at least for that week. She felt free as a bird and had no cares in the world! This was why she enjoyed motorcycling and someday she wanted to drive a bike of her own!

The trip was fun, but she was glad to return to her children, job, and home. Life was so much better for them than it had been!

Chandra returned home a day early so she could spend the day with her children before she had to go back to work. It was a warm August day, so the children were in the backyard playing in the sandbox while she sat and read the paper nearby. The lawnmower guy stopped by to see if maybe she wanted to go to the barbecue the landlord was having on Friday night. Chandra said she would see if she could get a sitter. Chandra also wanted to make sure this guy was decent, so she called her housing manager. She told Chandra that he was very nice and had a good sense of humor.

Chandra asked one of the neighbor girls to babysit, and they went to the barbecue. It was very nice. His name was Clyde. He had dark brown hair and green eyes, was 5'11", and was about 190 pounds. No drinking was involved. It was just laughter and fun! They stopped for a malt on the way home. It was very nice to have no alcohol involved, and they got along well. He said that he would call her again sometime soon.

A month passed, and no call.

Chandra was very disappointed. She had positive expectations that this might be the start of a nice relationship but then the bubble burst. It seemed to her that men were just there to hurt or disappoint her. She realized then that she had herself to depend on and her children came first in her life.

Chandra was busy with work and doing fun things with her children. They would go to the area parks and swimming pools. She didn't have much money, so they tried to do events that were free. They also went to many garage sales in elaborate neighborhoods where she would buy name brand clothes for her children at very low prices!

Chandra's ex-husband was able to start visitation again. He still had to have a relative with him as a supervisor. He was still on probation for the next five years, but he could still have visitation. Chandra did not understand this. She was worried every time the children left and said many prayers for their safe return.

They had to meet him at a public place. Chandra chose Perkins since many cops frequented the place for lunch and supper breaks.

Chandra packed a suitcase with their clothes and toothbrushes the first time they left for visitation for the weekend. He brought the children back with one of his relatives along, entered Perkins, threw the suitcase at Chandra as she sat in the waiting area, and shouted that he didn't need it!

Two policemen left their booth and asked if there was a problem. They looked at both children who were wearing the same clothes as when they left on Friday. They were both very dirty, and their hair was uncombed. They even had a stench to them. Chandra told the policemen that everything was okay. She never sent a suitcase again.

However, she did call the probation officer the next morning and reported the incident. She called the probation officer many times over the course of the years since the children were not in car seats or buckled in securely. He often brought them back at least a half hour late, too, which caused Chandra to be very nervous. She said many prayers at many times and thank goodness someone was listening.

Chandra also had the lyrics of the song "One Day at a Time" by Marilyn Sellars posted on her bathroom mirror as a reminder to herself to take one day at a time. Chandra's son was always nervous to go with his dad since he told her they were often left alone on the farm. Chandra gave her son the phone number of the sheriff's office since there was still no 911 for emergencies. Chandra told the probation officer this was happening and also called her attorney. They said that they needed proof to do anything or they would have to wait until something happened, which was not a good situation. If she did not let the children go for visitation, she would be held in contempt of court. Her son was very insecure and always wanted to be right by her side.

After visitations with their dad, the children would have injuries. Her son had a third degree burn from riding on a four-wheeler, and another time her daughter had an infected broken toe from her dad dropping a U-clamp on it. Neither injury was cared for by him.

Chandra would have to bring them to the doctor the next day to get medicine to treat the injuries. She also had to explain their injuries when social services called her since the children were on medical assistance. They thought that Chandra could be injuring the children, so she had to explain the story to them that the injuries happened while they were visiting their dad. This is why Chandra reported all incidents to the probation officer so they would have it recorded. Chandra also kept a journal of her own.

Chandra had picked up her son and daughter at Perkins after the weekend visitation with their father and decided to go to the grocery store. In the store, Chandra was asking what kind of cereal they wanted, telling them which ones were healthier for them, and her daughter of two years replied in her tiny, meek little voice by saying, "What do you know, straw head?"

Chandra looked at her with that mom-like look and asked, "What did you just call me?" She said in her meek little voice once again, "Straw head. That's what Daddy calls you."

Chandra then proceeded to tell both children, "I don't call him names; he should not be calling me names. It is not nice to call anyone names."

After weekend visitations on the first and third weekends of the month, it took Chandra a couple of days to get the children back on track, so they felt like they were back in their routine again. She still never understood why he got visitation, but the courts seemed to like both parents involved until a tragedy would happen. Chandra always prayed that the higher power would keep them safe and that their father would never harm them.

With an unlisted phone number, an inability to contact her old friends for herself and her children's safety, and living in a larger city than she was used to, Chandra felt a bit lonely. She was so grateful to have her children and nice coworkers.

Then, one night after supper, there was a knock on her door. Chandra didn't know enough people in this city to have visitors. She was terrified that it could be her abusive ex-husband, so she peeked through the curtains to see who it was.

It was Clyde, the lawnmower guy. Chandra was pretty cool towards him. He wondered why she wasn't happy to see him. Chandra stated that she had not heard from him for a couple of months and did not like to be treated that way. He said that he still wanted to date her, so she told him not to forget to call her. Clyde promised he wouldn't stand her up again.

Chandra had told herself when she left her ex-husband that she did not have to be treated badly anymore by anyone.

Clyde was enrolled in college. Chandra's second dream was to go to college. She lived in a college town, so maybe she should take a chance.

Chandra was a teller at a bank, and there was no advancement for her unless she wanted to move to a larger city, which she did not want to do. Her younger brother had moved in with her, and the duplex was too small, so they moved into a bigger house. Her niece was also starting college, so she moved in with them. Chandra started checking into grants for single parents and other financial aid. She decided to quit her job at the bank and attend college in the fall of 1987.

She ran into an old friend from vocational school who was looking for a place to live, so she moved in with them. Her niece had decided to move out with a friend to live closer to the college. Chandra's younger brother had a friend looking for a place to rent, so he also moved in. People that Chandra knew said that she had a commune going!

It worked out well since everyone had their own room. Chandra's brother and her worked days. Their friends worked evenings. Everyone was paying reasonable rent! She thought, *Where there is a will, there is a way!*

Chandra sold her new car, bought a used, less expensive car, and received AFDC and food stamps. She also remained on the sliding fee daycare. Chandra knew that government funding wasn't going to be her lifestyle forever. She just needed help to receive a two-year associate's degree to hopefully get better paying jobs.

Going to college gave her more time with her children than she did when she was working. She would do her studies after she put the children to bed at 8 p.m. The house they were renting was sold, so everyone had to find different housing. Chandra moved to a low-income townhome that was nice and closer to the college.

She did not take classes during the summer session, so she babysat for her sister and a neighbor while they were attending summer sessions at the college so she could be with her children more. Chandra lived by a park with a wading pool, so taking the children there daily was great when the weather was nice. Summertime was lots of fun. They had picnics in the park, played at area parks, and enjoyed walks.

Fall came and back to college she went. Her son went back to school and her daughter back to daycare. Chandra graduated Summa Cum Laude Spring of 1989 with an Associate of Arts Degree. This increased her self-esteem since she was abused so severely by her ex-husband. She had felt about two inches high after she left him. Now she felt her 5'4" height and held her head high for her achievement!

She did not feel stupid anymore. Look what she had accomplished! She was very grateful, and life was going on the right road.

Her life on this road was going straight and looking great!

Part 3

The Crooked Road

CHAPTER 13

Earl's family had accused Chandra that his drinking was her fault. But karma happened, and in August 1988, he was charged with a DUI. Again, in December 1990, he was charged with a DUI. Both times, he was on the Huber Law during the week and had to have relatives drive him to get the children for supervised visitation. He was definitely on the curvy road, while Chandra's road was straight and smooth.

Chandra had also received a certified letter for foreclosure on the farm she had lived on with him. She sent a copy of the quitclaim deed since she was no longer responsible for that farm. She didn't hear any more about that.

She was so glad that she had washed her hands of that farm years ago. With the children going on visitation twice a month and every other holiday, Chandra did not like Christmas as much as she used to. The holidays when she didn't have the children were very sad for her. Chandra would sit home alone during some holidays and cry. This was not what her life was supposed to be like. She was supposed to have a fairy tale marriage. She was feeling depressed. She did not like feeling this way. This wasn't her. She had lost herself. She needed to find herself again and start getting out in the community. So, she began to research where she could volunteer for holiday meals.

The city where she was living had many opportunities to volunteer. When she didn't have the children for holidays, she would go to one of the area churches and help serve holiday meals. This way she wasn't alone, and she felt like when she helped others, it gave her a very fulfilling feeling of happiness.

She also contacted the local women's shelter when the children were on weekend visitations with their dad to help volunteer. She went on a Saturday to help answer the phones. After listening and getting information from women who had called in and were in very bad abusive relationships, Chandra started feeling nauseous. The abuse that she had suffered and the terrible events that had occurred kept returning to her mind. She started to feel faint and could not think any more. She told the director of the women's shelter that she needed to leave. She was very sorry, but she could not endure listening to these stories of abuse anymore.

Chandra felt like she should have been stronger. It had been four years since she had left her abusive situation. She had completed counseling. Why wasn't she able to shake these terrible memories? She was in a wonderful relationship with Clyde so why did these terrible nightmares still haunt her?

CHAPTER 14

Clyde and Chandra had been dating for four years. They had taken trips to many places, did triathlons together, went fishing, swimming, and visiting relatives or friends on the weekends. They liked to do physical activities together, listen to music, and they had great families. Clyde asked Chandra to marry him. She said yes because this relationship felt right.

Her lease was up in May. She was getting married in August, so she asked her older sister if she and her children could live with her until the wedding. This worked well since she could watch their children while her sister taught summer school.

After the wedding, Clyde and Chandra discussed buying some lake property. Chandra had a third dream of living on a lake someday.

Then, one night, as she was reading the *Sunday Tribune*, Chandra noticed an ad for a log home for sale on a lake about sixty miles away. Chandra talked it over with Clyde, and they called the number in the ad.

A man answered the phone and said that he had just bought an old resort that had been closed for years. He was sectioning off the land so the house would be for sale. There were also five cabins, a lodge, and thirty campsites. Of these campsites, twelve were full hookups, and eighteen were remote, with some that had electricity. He was splitting off the land to sell in parcels. Right now, he was just interested in selling the log home with a tuck-under garage on one hundred feet of lakeshore for $55,000. They set up an appointment to meet with him on the following Saturday.

It was springtime, and there was still snow on the ground and ice on the lake. He told them that there was a sand bottom where reeds were poking through the ice. They could see reeds poking through where the swimming beach was, so they took his word for it. He wanted a ten thousand dollar down payment and a contract for deed for the log home. Clyde and Chandra had five thousand dollars cash, but he wasn't very happy about that amount. He said that they could trash the place. It would then cost a lot more than that to repair. Reluctantly, he accepted that amount.

Chandra was excited. Her dream of living on a lake was becoming a reality! She was giddy and could not wait for the move!

They were letting the children finish school where they lived. Both Clyde and Chandra continued working in the area. They went to the lake house on the weekends to clean the house and started moving items each time they went. They would move permanently to their home on the lake on Memorial Day weekend when the children finished school.

One weekend, when they were at the house, a man stopped to tell them that his parents owned the log home and resort. He was from Indiana. He wished he had the money to purchase it all since he missed the lake and the beautiful woods surrounding the resort. He proceeded to tell them that his father had shot himself in the bedroom and wanted to show them where the bullet hole was in the logs. They did let him in the house, and he showed them. He told them that after his father died, his mother was unable to maintain the resort. The bank had foreclosed on the resort. The cabins, lodge, and campground had been closed for eight years.

Chandra's cousin and his family ran a resort. She had taken her two children there for a week-long summer vacation a couple of times before she had met Clyde. They had a lot of fun swimming, fishing, and enjoying lake life for a week each summer. Chandra also helped them clean cabins and sell bait in their store.

This gave Chandra the idea to have her cousin and his wife come to see the log home that they were buying on the lake. Also, she wanted to get their opinion about whether to buy or run the rest of the resort. Chandra's cousins were excited to come to see the new adventure!

Her cousin told them that the cabins could be the bread and butter of the resort. These would make the most money as the lodge and camping would be less profitable. The cabins needed a lot of repairs, and Clyde was not a carpenter. Chandra's cousin thought she and Clyde should purchase the rest of the resort.

They talked with the owner of the resort the following weekend. His idea was to sell the cabins separately to other people and they lease the land from him. He did want the cabins painted since they were a deep barn red. He offered to pay Chandra to paint the cabins since she would not work that summer. This way, she was home with her children, who would start third and fifth grade in the fall.

They also worked it out to open the campground and put some games in the lodge. They were on the way to becoming resort managers! Even though they weren't exactly sure what they were doing. They were moving to a new area with no jobs and becoming resort owners, a job which they knew little about.

Chandra wondered where this road was taking them. Was it going to be straight or curvy?

CHAPTER 15

The first summer was a rainy one. Chandra would be outside painting one of the cabins, come in to have lunch, and a down pouring of rain would come. The paint all washed off in a matter of minutes. This happened a lot. They didn't have good weather predictions back then.

Also, tent campers would come on the weekends and get rained out. Chandra would feel so bad that she would refund their money. It took a while to build up the news that the campground was reopened after years of being closed. They had to cut down many trees that had overgrown the camping areas. The beach was very weedy, so they rented a weed roller to clear it. They also used dirt rakes to manually pull weeds, bottles, cans, and old dock sections out of the lake. It took a lot of labor to get it looking good!

They also had very reasonable rates for seasonal and weekend campsites. They were chamber members, talked to other campgrounds and said that if they were filled to send them their direction, and did newspaper advertising to bring in business.

Chandra and Clyde were both busy filling out job applications in the area. By the fall of 1992, Clyde and Chandra had both been hired by the nearby public school. He was a teacher's aide in the high school, and she was a teacher's aide in the elementary school.

Chandra had applied for the school's district office bookkeeper position but did not get that job. Chandra was grateful to have the teacher's aide position since it gave her the summer off to run the campground. Her husband also had the summer off but got part-time jobs to help with the bills as the campground wasn't very profitable at first.

These were good times to live the lake life! Chandra's third dream had come true! Chandra thought the children enjoyed helping with the campground. Chandra did know that they enjoyed swimming, fishing, tubing, canoeing, and paddle boating during the week when the campground wasn't as busy. Her daughter had a favorite tree by the lodge that she would climb and read a book.

What better view than to look out and see the lake? Chandra loved looking out the window each morning to see the lake. She could hear the loons too.

They met so many great people when they were managing the campground. But after a few years, the shower house and the lodge needed maintenance. The owner was supposed to handle these maintenance issues, but he wasn't. The road was getting curvy with him.

He then suggested that they purchase the campground and lodge from him instead of sharing it with him. They decided to do it, then they would get all the profit! He fixed the maintenance problems first, and then they became the owners.

The campground was filled with seasonal campers, and the weekend sites were filled. The owner's cabins that he wanted sold were not doing so well. Only one cabin was sold to an older couple from Illinois. They were very nice people. The owner wanted Chandra and Clyde to show the cabins and said that he would give them a small fee for it. When Chandra showed the cabins, they were unfurnished. This did not help them sell. So, the owner decided to sell the other four cabins to a couple from the neighboring town that Clyde and Chandra knew as acquaintances.

This couple thought that they could run the resort together. The wife had coffee cups made with the resort's name but only listed their phone number. Chandra was not too impressed by this. Chandra and Clyde had been in a partnership before this, and it did not work out well. Chandra did not want another partnership, so she told them she and Clyde would run their campground and lodge. Then, the other couple would be responsible for their three cabins as they would live in the biggest of the four cabins.

The lodge was not earning Clyde and Chandra a lot since most games would break down. The company that owned them would not come to fix them very fast. They decided to turn the lodge into a year-round cabin. Chandra cashed in a ten thousand dollar IRA, so they would have money to do this.

They constructed some walls and a bathroom. Chandra bought furniture from a second-hand store for the living room and kitchen as well as bed frames for the bedrooms. They purchased new mattresses for the bed frames. The cabin was able to sleep eight people! They had very low rates to start with just to get business.

This did not sit well with their new neighbors, who had three cabins to rent, since they were charging more. Clyde and Chandra's philosophy was that business is business, and to get business, start low to fill the cabin. After a while, rates could always increase.

Clyde and Chandra's business was going well! The road was straight and smooth. The neighbors with the cabins were on the other side of the road. They had a Chesapeake dog that was not very friendly. He was very intimidating as he would run forcefully toward people. He was not a good resort dog to have running loose. After three separate instances of campers being trapped on the dock by their dog, the dog chased campers, and the last straw was when a young boy was bitten by the dog while riding his bike.

The sheriff's department issued them a letter stating the dog had to be put down or given away to someone who does not have a public business. The owners of the cabins gave the Chesapeake dog to a farmer who lived five miles away and, after a couple of years, sold the cabins to four other people. They were going to have these as their summer vacation homes.

This made the road straight and smooth to run the campground and cabin rentals! There were many, many campground stories that Chandra could share, but that might have to be the next book!

CHAPTER 16

Since Chandra's parents didn't travel much with their children, she wanted to travel with her children so they could see more than the only towns they lived in. They drove to West Virginia when her nephew lived there. On the way, they visited the Football Hall of Fame in Canton, Ohio, and Washington D.C. sites. Then they traveled south to Virginia Beach and Nashville, Tennessee. They went to Opryland and did many fun rides! They also saw a guitar player standing on the corner, and his name was Travis Tritt. They had never heard of him. Within a few years, he became a famous country western singer. They traveled to Sturgis, South Dakota, to the motorcycle rally with many memories. Some were rated R! They also went to Denver, Colorado to visit a sister-in-law, where they enjoyed skiing in the mountains. Chandra guessed her older son did not enjoy skiing so much as he ended up in the parking lot from the bunny hill since he could not stop! He then decided to sit in the lodge and drink hot cocoa while they continued skiing.

Like every parent, you think you must take your children to Disney World in Florida, so Chandra did! The children were older, so they thought they were too old for Small World but as they traveled along in the little boat on the river, they were fascinated with how all of it worked. Epcot Center and MGM studios were their favorites.

Chandra's two sisters and her also traveled together after the oldest sister died. They went on trips to New York City, Branson, Missouri, Black Hills, and South Dakota wine trips. Seattle, Washington, Oregon, and Great Falls, Montana. They wanted to take a sister trip every year, but life happens when you have children and work, so they went on trips when they could. Clyde would also take trips with his brother or other guy friends. It was nice that way since they trusted each other.

When they traveled as a family, they did not spend much money. Sometimes, they slept in the van, on a trampoline in the waitress' backyard from a local restaurant, or just rolled out sleeping bags onto bare ground! They also stayed with relatives or friends. They packed snacks and beverages instead of eating at restaurants.

Chandra still enjoys traveling and wants to explore more places. There are many places on her Bucket List!

She would like to travel to Hawaii, Alaska, California, Maine and European countries.

It was tricky taking trips in the summer as owners of a campground and cabin, so many of the trips happened at other times of the year. Chandra's two children were a great help with the campground! They mowed the lawn and cleaned the shower house and cabin. Clyde worked odd jobs during the summer. When he wasn't working, he enjoyed lying in the sun. The lake was great, but it was very busy!

Every weekend they had relatives coming to enjoy the lake life. Their lives on the weekends became like a party. Having campers and relatives enjoying alcoholic beverages, fishing, swimming, bonfires, and playing volleyball and basketball. Chandra and Clyde would also be drinking and enjoying good times when all the campers were checked in. They enjoyed entertaining but sometimes one or the other of them would overindulge. This started creating a few problems in their marriage.

The road was getting a bit curvy.

Chandra was getting worried that this marriage was not going to work. She felt overwhelmed with work, running the resort, and keeping up with everything in the house.

CHAPTER 17

Then, suddenly, when Chandra's children were fourteen and eleven, Clyde wanted to have a child of their own. They were thirty-seven years old!

Chandra wasn't so sure about this. She was not sure how she would manage more responsibility but she thought that she would have plenty of help from her husband and felt that she needed to let him be a father to a child of his own.

After a few months, Chandra went to the doctor to have a pregnancy test; they didn't have home tests at this time. The test was positive. Her daughter had come with her, but she did not tell her the reason why she was at the doctor's office.

Chandra was excited and could not wait to get home to tell Clyde!

When they came home, she found Clyde, and they went to another room to talk privately.

Chandra said with enthusiasm, "We are going to have a baby!"

Clyde looked at her with a frown and said, "What?"

He did not seem very happy.

Chandra was very confused. This was his idea! He might have been shocked. Clyde then smiled and said, "This is wonderful news!"

He hugged Chandra and they went to the kitchen to tell the older children. They were all excited to be welcoming another one to their family!

They had to make some changes in their home to make room for the baby that would be born in August. So, the office became a nursery. They also had to buy a crib, changing table, and other baby items, but the transition was easy. Chandra borrowed maternity clothes from a friend since she knew this would be the last child that she had.

The doctor was a bit nervous because of her age, so he wanted to do amniocentesis. She declined this procedure since she knew that she would accept the baby with loving arms whether they had any physical abnormalities or not.

The campground was busy! They were getting ready for the holiday weekend of the fourth of July 1996 with a full campground, cabin, and a few relatives coming to stay with them in their house, along with having a basketball tournament at the campground.

At 4:30 a.m. on July 3, Chandra went to the bathroom, and as she was walking back to the bedroom, her water broke! She called the hospital, and they said that she would need to come in since she would have to have the baby within the next twenty-four hours, either naturally or have a C section. Clyde stated that he needed to shower first.

Chandra thought, *Really?*

After his shower, they drove to the local hospital twelve miles from their home. Chandra wasn't having any contractions, so the nurse wanted her to walk through the halls to get things moving.

Chandra told herself that she was going to have the baby by noon.

Her contractions started, and a cute baby boy was born at 12:36 p.m. Their son was turning blue with labored breathing. The doctor quickly called to get him to a larger hospital ninety miles away. The nurse used a straw-like tube with air flowing, positioning it by his nostrils, and her hand was shaking. Chandra touched her hand gently, saying that she knew he would be all right. Chandra was not sure why she was so calm, but she felt the presence of a higher power helping everyone.

So, their newborn son was whisked away to another state.

Chandra felt empty. She had just had a baby but did not even get to hold him. She wanted to get out of the hospital now!

She wanted to be with her newborn baby boy. But she was still in the hospital, and the doctor said that he would check her at 6 p.m. to see if she would be able to be discharged. What an awful feeling to have a baby, and then it is taken away.

So 6 p.m. came, and the doctor said that everything looked good. The doctor then released Chandra from the hospital. Chandra hurriedly dressed and was ready for the drive! She and Clyde were on their way to the hospital to be with their newborn son!

Chandra's older children were with their father for the week. Earl did get one week per year in the summer for visitation. He was not on probation anymore.

When they arrived at the hospital, they went to the Neonatal Intensive Care Unit. Many tiny babies were in incubators with tubes attached. Their son had his hands duct taped to the side of the incubator with an oxygen tube in his nostrils. They had to duct tape his hands down since he kept pulling the tube out. Chandra knew he was a fighter!

What had happened to their baby was that he had swallowed amniotic fluid. After they suctioned out the fluid, his lungs were fine.

Chandra was so thankful that he would be okay, even though she knew he would be okay from the beginning.

They did not have cell phones then, so they purchased a long-distance calling card to use the hospital phone to call relatives. The policy in NICU was they had to stay a minimum of four days, and only six other visitors besides the parents would be able to come to see him for the whole time that he might be there. Clyde's mother, her two daughters, and Chandra's sister came to visit.

Clyde and Chandra left the other two spots open for Chandra's son and daughter in case he had to stay longer than the four days.

They also had to call a cousin who would be visiting over July 4th to ask him to run the campground and tell people that the basketball tournament was canceled. Clyde and Chandra stayed at the Ronald McDonald House, which was very inexpensive and had a kitchen where they could prepare their own food. They were at the hospital most of the day but watched fireworks outside on Independence Day.

On July 7th, they could leave the hospital with their little firecracker. Chandra felt bad for the other parents of the babies in the NICU who had been there so long, and they were able to leave after a few days.

Chandra felt very grateful that the road had turned out straight and smooth for them. She was so excited to get her little boy home!

Her older children returned home a few days later. They were so helpful taking care of their little brother. Life was busy with two teenagers and a baby, but Chandra wouldn't have changed it for the world!

Since their baby was six weeks early, Chandra was not prepared. Chandra had switched from being a teacher's aide to an administrative assistant. She was working in the district office at the school, and many reports were due. Auditors were coming, and supplies needed to be ordered for the school year for the teachers' purchase orders. Her coworker brought the Annual Transportation Report to her home so she could complete it in her spare time. She brought her young son to school so that while he slept, she could complete other work. All the deadlines were met, but Chandra was exhausted!

She had asked her husband if she could ask for a leave of absence for a year, but he said they couldn't afford it. The first year of her son's life was a bit tough since he woke up every two hours to be fed. Chandra felt like a zombie going to work, coming home to make meals, cleaning, doing laundry, and going to her other children's activities.

She would ask her husband to help her with some of the household duties or to get up with their son during the night so she could get some rest, but he had been telling people for months before the birth that nothing in life would change when the baby was born.

Chandra thought that many things would change.

Many people gave him an odd look when he said this. Chandra always told him that there would be changes. She realized that he thought his life wouldn't change, and actually it didn't. Thank goodness her older children pitched in and watched their brother and helped around the house.

When the following summer rolled around, her daughter babysat her younger brother while Chandra worked two miles away at the school from Monday to Thursday. Her older son helped with the outside by mowing the campground and taking campground/cabin reservations. They always teased Chandra about the chore lists she would write for them daily. They told her that they would wait until about an hour before she got home to do the chores on the list, but they always got things done!

Chandra was very appreciative of that.

CHAPTER 18

They made many years of wonderful memories at the lake. Clyde and Chandra met so many nice people while they owned the campground and cabin. However, as time passed and her older children were graduating from high school and spreading their wings, she just couldn't do it alone. Her youngest son was six, and her husband, as said before, was not very helpful with the campground or other chores. Chandra needed to give herself a break from all the work. Clyde was more interested in riding his Harley Davidson motorcycle and keeping fit than anything else. The road was getting a bit curvy again.

Their youngest son was very active, which kept them all on their toes! He had many nicknames since he liked to play in the dirt. They called him "Pigpen" from Charlie Brown. He would also have toys all over the room in a few seconds so he seemed like the cartoon character "Tasmanian Devil" who would twirl around like a tornado.

He always said funny comments. One time, when they were trying to put an item together, he said that they needed the "constructions" instead of instructions. He was also very good at playing hide and seek since he stayed so quiet, but it was scary since they lived by a lake, woods, and highway. One time he was found underneath the deck of the cabin when his dad was supposed to be watching him. He was a quick little fellow! One minute he was there and the next he had disappeared! Since he was almost like an only child, he had imaginary friends. He kept himself very entertained. He would also play with the neighbor boy who also had much older siblings. They got along really well. The neighbor boy became like another son to Chandra. Chandra and Clyde would still take time to do things with friends and hire a babysitter. In June 2001, Clyde and Chandra drove their motorcycle to a birthday party for one of their friends that started at the town liquor store for a couple of drinks and then they were going to go to dinner. Their friend's daughter was babysitting at their house. Everyone had a few drinks when a few of their motorcycle friends came into the liquor store. Clyde decided he would leave to go on a ride with these friends. Chandra said that they were supposed to go to dinner for the birthday party, but Clyde left on his motorcycle instead.

Chandra still kept smiling and enjoying her friends, but she was very upset that Clyde had deserted her.

He knew where they were going to dinner, so Chandra thought he might ride for a while and meet them at the restaurant. Chandra ended up riding with her friends to the restaurant. Everyone had a wonderful dinner with lots of fun and laughter. Clyde never showed up, so her friends drove Chandra home. They came inside to pick up their daughter, who had been babysitting. The babysitter told Chandra that Clyde had called, and he was in jail for a DUI. The road was getting curvier!

The next morning, Clyde was released and came home. Needless to say, Chandra was not very happy. He paid his fines, and he went on with his life. They were still running the campground but had decided to put it up for sale along with their cabin. The realtor said that if it sold, they also might want to buy their house, so they should have a plan.

They had an extra lot and they looked into building a house or getting a modular home to put on a foundation. The lot was just through the woods and up the hill from their house. They could see the other lake across the highway, so the view would be nice. They looked at modular homes, and they disagreed on what they wanted. They weren't getting along very well.

The realtor brought people out to check out the campground and cabin, but it was not selling. They thought about converting the whole campground to seasonal sites to ease up some of the work and have each seasonal mow their own lot. It would have cost quite a bit of money, so they decided against this idea since they didn't want more debt.

Clyde's uncle was an auctioneer, so in early September of 2002, they had an auction. Two people were bidding. They knew them both. Some neighbors were also at the auction just to see the outcome. One of the bidders just wanted the campground, and the other bidder wanted the cabin. This worked out very well for everyone!

Chandra decided to stop working full-time at the school since they paid off all of their debt by selling the campground and cabin. She needed a break. It was nice to be at home to do housework during the day and not feel pressured about preparing meals since she could take the whole day to plan what to cook.

Later, in September 2002, Clyde and Chandra were invited to a wedding in the neighboring town. Clyde had been drinking two-fisted Jack Daniels drinks all night at the reception. Chandra had a few drinks but had been dancing quite a bit, so she felt pretty sober. When it was time to leave, Chandra wanted to drive, but Clyde would not give her the keys.

She got into the passenger front seat, and he got into the driver's seat. They had parked by the brick building, so he needed to back up and leave the parking spot. He put the car in drive! He almost hit the building, but Chandra screamed! He hit the brakes. Chandra then told him that she should be driving. He said that he was fine and was going to drive.

They exited the parking spot and got onto the highway heading out of town. Clyde was going over the center line and then swerving back into the lane.

Chandra was thinking that they might get into an accident, and she began to panic. Within a mile, there were cop lights behind them. Clyde pulled over to the side of the road. Some friends were ahead of them in a vehicle and saw the cop lights, so they pulled over. The cop approached the driver's side, asking Clyde for his driver's license and insurance information.

The friends ended up turning around to see what was happening. The cop then called for backup since he thought these friends were up to no good. The cop ran Clyde's record and discovered that this was his second offense, so the vehicle would be impounded.

After the cop realized that these friends who had turned around didn't mean any harm, he asked if Chandra could ride home with them.

Chandra was so relieved that they were there for her!

Clyde was taken to jail, the vehicle was impounded, and she was home safe with her son. She was not very happy with her husband. If she would have been driving, he would not have been in this mess! It was getting so out of control! It was a very, very curvy road.

Chandra was thinking that this seemed like déjà vu with her first marriage, but she was very glad that there was no abuse.

The next morning, Clyde called and said that Chandra could come and pick him up. Chandra said that things needed to change, so she wouldn't pick him up until he told her what he would change in his life so maybe their marriage would not be so rocky.

Chandra thought selling the campground would relieve her stress, but she realized that it might be her husband who was the problem!

Clyde told Chandra on the phone that he would stop drinking. Chandra said that she would stop drinking too. She took her son to the pickup truck to head to the jail to pick up his dad. Oh boy, what a thing their young son had to go through!

She felt so sorry for putting another child through marital problems. Why was marriage so difficult for her?

This second offense required Clyde to attend group therapy sessions and to put whiskey plates on Chandra's car. After driving him to these group sessions and driving around with whiskey plates a few times, Chandra felt like she was being punished!

Chandra had attended Teen Anon when her parents were drinking and Al-Anon when Earl and her younger brother had to participate in Alcoholics Anonymous. She learned about "tough love" in these programs, so sometimes, it was hard for her to be empathetic.

She finally said he needed someone else to drive him to these sessions. He also had to figure out how to pay his fine. Their relationship was tense, to say the least.

Chandra started doing things on her own with her son. Chandra also took a weekend motorcycle class and got her license. She then bought her own motorcycle trike so she could take her son with her whenever they wanted to go riding.

She started planning to get her son through school, and when he graduated, she would file for divorce. She didn't want to put another child through divorce. Chandra thought that it was not a straight, smooth road right now!

One night, Clyde told Chandra he was attracted to the married neighbor lady. Chandra was shocked that he would even tell her this!

What husband says this to his wife?

Needless to say, this did not help their relationship at all. The married neighbor lady would even call their house and ask for him. Chandra told the neighbor lady's husband about this, but he just shrugged it off. This couple got divorced a few years later.

CHAPTER 19

Chandra had started working at three part-time jobs so she could start saving money. She also was a member of the school board that her son attended. She was very organized with files per day per job as to what she had to do when she got to work.

On the school board, she was there for the people and returned phone calls to concerned taxpayers to give them answers and solve problems. Her old job as a district office bookkeeper was open for applications. She quit all three part-time jobs and applied for her old position since she was working forty hours per week without benefits with these other jobs.

Chandra took a chance quitting these other jobs before she found out if she would be rehired. If they didn't hire her, she would be unemployed again. She received the good news a couple of days later that she would be returning to her position as Administrative Assistant in the district office.

She was ecstatic that they decided to rehire her! It would be easy to come back since she knew the position and what it entailed!

Chandra asked to work ten months and have two months off in the summer so she could be home with her son. The school board and superintendent agreed to this arrangement.

A new superintendent had been hired since she worked there last. He seemed to work very well with the office personnel. He seemed very pleasant and easy to get along with. Most of the staff got along fine with him but there are always a few that don't get along with anyone.

Chandra resigned from the school board since she was a school employee once again. She had helped hire this superintendent when she was a school board member, even though another school district had not renewed his contract due to problems he caused at that district. Chandra's older son lived in the same area as this superintendent and said he was a good person, but the school district did not want to renew his contract for some unknown reason.

Chandra worked full time and was involved in many activities with her son, who was in Boy Scouts, football, basketball, and golf. She was a member of the PTA and volunteered with many activities in the community. She kept busy and did very little with her husband. The romance had ended years ago, and the road was very curvy.

One day while Chandra was having lunch in the teacher's lounge with other staff, Clyde came in and said very loudly, "How's everyone's libido today?"

Chandra was so embarrassed and wished she could have slid under the table to hide! All the staff looked at him and their jaws dropped open. Nobody said a word. Clyde gave a nervous chuckle and left the room.

Chandra felt like everyone in the room was looking at her and she felt like an idiot! But why should she? Being in a relationship it felt like the other person was a part of her. When they said something, it seemed like it reflected on her. But why was this?

In the summer of 2009, Chandra could not deal with her marriage anymore. She felt that her husband was having an affair, but she didn't care anymore. Chandra started the divorce papers and hired a lawyer.

Chandra did tell some of the school staff that she was divorcing her husband. Clyde had gotten rehired by the school as a bus mechanic since, in 1994, the school superintendent had forced him to resign as a high school teacher's aide since he had been going to student parties, is what he told Chandra.

When Chandra told the staff, one of them sunk into a chair. The staff member pulled her aside to a private area where two other staff members were present. Chandra then found out why her husband had to resign in 1994. He had been writing notes to a young female high school student to have a rendezvous with him and attend student parties. The parents took Clyde to court, and he was ordered to stay away from the female student and not be in the school building except for public events.

The school bus garage was two miles away, so that is why they rehired him as a bus mechanic. He would not be around any students at the bus garage.

Chandra was shocked to hear this information! This incident had happened when they had only been married five years!

She felt very hurt. She had trusted her husband.

Chandra approached him about this using the paperwork the parents gave her. He told Chandra that this young female student had come on to him.

Chandra thought, *What part of this doesn't he understand?*

The parents didn't want to tell Chandra about this when it happened, and it was kept very quiet. The parents didn't want to be the reason that Chandra would divorce Clyde. Chandra would have appreciated knowing the truth even though it wouldn't have been any easier on her.

These facts deeply hurt her. Chandra still felt strongly that Clyde was having an affair too.

She confronted him. "Are you having an affair?"

Clyde looked away from Chandra not looking her in the eyes and said, "No." So, Chandra knew that he was lying since he couldn't even look her in the eyes when he said that he wasn't having an affair.

She told him, "I don't care who it was, but I know that there is someone else."

A married staff member came to Chandra's office and wanted to talk privately. He told Chandra that he had been following his wife and Clyde. He had seen them together many times. His wife was also a staff member at the school. This married couple also started divorce proceedings.

Wow! This road is crazy curvy!

CHAPTER 20

The superintendent that Chandra worked for treated her differently after the divorce. He accused her of doing terrible things. She started keeping a journal of dates, times, and incidents when the superintendent made other remarks that were demeaning to her. Chandra sent these items to her lawyer since she had told some school board members about what was happening to her and they did nothing. She felt she had to go further. Chandra told the school board members that she had hired a lawyer. They still didn't seem to care. Other staff members had heard the remarks he made to Chandra, so they put these incidents in writing.

In May of 2010, a taxpayer brought to Chandra's attention that one of the school board members had his personal vehicle in the school bus garage, and her ex-husband was working on his vehicle. She knew the government rules, and this was not allowed. Chandra emailed the superintendent and all school board members to let them know about this incident. She would be as guilty as they were at breaking government rules if she did not report it. She received an answer by email from the board member who had his vehicle in the school bus garage. This incident leaked to the local paper, and many taxpayers became angry. The superintendent reprimanded the school board member. The superintendent and school board members acted like this was no big deal, and Chandra was out for vengeance.

She could not believe that they were saying this. She was just doing her job! In June of 2010, representatives of the Local Federation of Teachers Union had a Meet and Confer session to discuss concerns regarding the lack of leadership in the school district and they had made numerous attempts to the school board. A survey had been completed. Within ten minutes of the meeting, the superintendent was disgusted with what he was hearing and left the room. After a few more minutes, the school board members left the room. After a while, one of the school board members returned, informing the group that they were on a conference call with legal counsel. The meeting ended without a further presentation from the faculty to the board regarding the survey results. This superintendent and board were very much getting out of control! They were going on a very curvy road!

In August of 2010, Chandra's older son recognized a school vehicle with a trailer and a car on the trailer at the superintendent's home. He took pictures. He then sent this information to one of the school board members. They sent an email to him stating all kinds of reasons why the superintendent was allowed to use a government vehicle.

The next day, the superintendent and a school board member called Chandra into the office to meet with them. She said she would not meet without her lawyer since she would not endure another closed-door meeting alone—especially two against one!

She picked up the phone to call her lawyer, but the superintendent said she was fired and told her to turn in her keys! Chandra asked, "On what grounds?"

He stated, "For insubordination."

Chandra asked him to put that in writing. He did.

As she packed up her items, she felt relief. Chandra had been applying for other jobs since working around her ex-husband and his girlfriend was stressful. Chandra's coworker hugged her tight. Chandra had worked in that office for a total of fifteen years! How could this be happening to her? She was a dedicated employee!

The superintendent and school board thought she was a troublemaker, but she did excellent work, and she knew the law. She was not trying to cause problems. After she left the school that day, her coworker told her that the school board member had told her to think of someone who could come in to help her since the start of school was the busiest time ever. She told the school board member that this job was complicated, and you must have accounting experience. Chandra felt so sorry for her coworker since it was such a busy time for this to happen, and it would take time for someone to learn all the aspects of Chandra's position.

Chandra contacted her lawyer as soon as she was home. The house still had not sold. She still had to make payments. She knew that she needed a job, but at this point, she just needed to breathe.

Chandra felt relief from leaving a stressful environment, but she was also feeling stressed since she did not know what her future held. She still had a son to raise and payments to make. Now she was out of a good paying job. The curves in the road were getting wicked!

A few days later, the local newspaper called and wanted to interview her about her paid leave of absence. Chandra told them that she had been fired. They had already interviewed the school administration and they told the reporter that Chandra was on a paid leave of absence.

This was good news! At least she was still getting paid!

A public meeting was going to be held regarding her dismissal. Chandra contacted all the people she knew so they could attend this meeting to support her. Many people said that they would attend the meeting: her family, staff members, and the public.

A few days later, the meeting was canceled by the school administration. She figured that they heard about the crowd coming to the meeting.

She felt disappointed that the meeting was canceled. Now she had to deal with the school board and superintendent by herself. They had not been helpful in the past, so she wasn't feeling too confident they would be helpful now.

Chandra's older son was not happy about the superintendent dismissing his mom. He called the superintendent to vent his anger. A few days later, he got a call from the county sheriff's department that harassment charges had been filed against him. He called his mom, and she asked who he had talked to. Chandra knew that deputy sheriff. He was really good friends with the superintendent. Chandra asked her son if he could attend the next school board meeting in a few days. He said that he would be there. Chandra was also going to be in attendance.

The retired superintendent, who hired Chandra fifteen years ago, was also coming to the school board meeting along with a former school board member. One of the current school board members had written a letter to the editor claiming the school policies were not current, so that was why all of these laws were broken. They were not happy with that article since they wrote the current policies with Chandra's help following state statutes.

It was an interesting school board meeting! The auditor was there to present the past year's audit, which was fine. In all the years Chandra worked in the district office, the audit always came out wonderful!

But the meeting got heated, when Chandra's son explained that he stopped at the county courthouse to get the paperwork on the harassment filed by the superintendent, but there was no paperwork. All the board members turned their heads simultaneously in surprise to look at the superintendent! Apparently, they didn't know that he had done that!

The retired superintendent and former school board member also voiced their concerns that the policies they implemented were according to state statutes. The new administration and school board violated these policies. The auditor was taking note of all this. Items like this had to be reported to the state.

After a few weeks, an agreement was made with Chandra and the school district. They paid her eight weeks of severance pay to resign from the school, and she could claim unemployment benefits.

Many editorials in the paper were written and talked about how fishy this was since she was fired shortly after her son reported misuse of a government vehicle. Taxpayers were wondering why they needed to pay Chandra to resign from her position of fifteen years.

Chandra continued attending school board meetings since she still had a son attending school. It was really fun for her to stare down the board members. They would look down and not even look at her! Besides, she had nothing better to do since she was unemployed.

Chandra became employed again, and the house was finally sold. Her finances were looking good, and she was enjoying life. Chandra began renting the basement in a friend's home because she knew she would move out of the area once her son graduated high school.

One day, Chandra was reading the local paper during her lunch hour. In the paper was an article from the state auditor regarding the misuse of government buildings and vehicles by the school district superintendent and school board. She knew it wasn't legal but seeing it in black and white for the public to read was so nice!

Straight and smooth was the path she was on!

In March 2014, it was reported that a staff member had slapped a special needs elementary student while two teacher aides were restraining the child. The staff member was the superintendent who had dismissed Chandra in 2010. The superintendent got reprimanded and retired in June 2014. Another bit of karma was that Clyde and his girlfriend broke up after an eight-year relationship.

Part 4

The Freeway

CHAPTER 21

After each relationship Chandra would look at her reflection in the mirror and try to make improvements in her own behavior.

What could she have done differently? What could she have said that might have improved the relationship? It takes two to tango, right? There are always two sides to the story, as they say. Why was she failing at these relationships? She decided to take some time for herself and find the person that she wanted to be. She also started a pros and cons list in relationships. If the cons outweigh the pros, she moved on.

After a few months when Chandra had reflected and knew what she wanted in life, she decided to check out online dating since she had moved to a new community. She had a friend that gave her good advice about meeting up with someone:

1. Always meet in a public place.
2. Tell at least one person where you are going and when you expect to be home.
3. Never give out your address until you know the person seems harmless.

Chandra even started looking them up on the state public website for any crimes they may have committed.

Chandra met up to go to dinner or a movie with a few different men, but they didn't feel like they had much in common.

One night, Chandra was going to a dance class in the neighboring city with another single lady. She loved to dance, so she thought that it might be fun! She had been communicating with a guy on a dating site, and he lived in this city.

Chandra texted him to maybe meet him at the place where the dance class was held. It was a bar/restaurant, so they could visit and have a beverage together after the dance class. He texted back that he wasn't sure he could make it and that he wasn't dancing! Chandra told him it would be a good chance to meet and that he wouldn't have to dance. They could just sit in the bar and have a beer. She told him that she would really like to meet him, and it would be a good time to do this since she was headed to the city anyway for the evening. He texted back, stating that Chandra had quite the language! She was confused about what he meant by that, so she didn't text him anything back. He then texted her that he would meet her around 8 p.m. The dance class started at 7 p.m. so she let him know that 8 p.m. worked fine to meet him.

When he arrived, she stopped dancing, and they found a small table by the bar. He showed Chandra the text that she had sent him. *&^%$#*@!?+!@#$%&%? is what it looked like, so he thought she was swearing at him! Apparently, her Tracfone did not communicate with his iPhone! Needless to say, after they have been together for over nine years now, there is still some miscommunication sometimes! Just for the record, Chandra did buy an iPhone.

He didn't like to dance to fast dances, so many of her lady friends come to dance, and then he becomes the "purse watcher." When he and Chandra took a trip to South Padre Island, almost every bar they walked into played the song "Tennessee Whiskey" by David Allan Coe, George Jones, Chris Stapleton, or other artists that have also covered this song. Therefore, this has become their song. He would dance to that song since it was a "buckle shiner."

Chandra's journey was going straight and smooth, but on September 17, 2019, Chandra was driving to her boyfriend's house on I-35 so they could spend the weekend together. Signs were flashing for miles on the Interstate regarding roadwork ahead and to slow down.

The road had lots of traffic, but it was moving along at a safe speed. She saw many brake lights about a hundred feet ahead, and traffic slowed. Then, all of a sudden, all traffic was at a standstill, so she braked and stopped at a safe distance from the car in front of her.

She glanced in the rearview mirror, and a black pickup truck was coming at a fast speed right behind her! Chandra's eyes widened as she watched the pickup slam into her vehicle. She started spinning, spinning, spinning while pushing on the brakes and trying to stop the spinning.

She thought that she was going to die! Her life flashed in front of her eyes. She did not want to die! She had so much to live for!

She started to slide backwards. She still tried to stop by pushing the brakes, but nothing happened. She kept sliding backwards. Then, all of a sudden, there was a crash at the back of her vehicle. She had stopped. She was alive! The back end of her vehicle was up against the guardrail. Chandra grabbed her phone and dialed 911. She started to tell them about the accident, but the dispatcher stopped her by saying that help was already on the way.

Within seconds, a police officer was by her vehicle, asking if she was okay. Chandra was definitely shaken up and probably in shock as she handed him her driver's license and insurance information. The fire truck arrived, and the firemen told her to exit her vehicle in case it started on fire.

Chandra got out of the vehicle with wobbly legs and looked around. Her vehicle was totally smashed on the rear passenger side and the exhaust was lying on the ground. The black pickup was in front of her against the guardrail with his front driver's side smashed.

A woman stopped to see if Chandra was okay. She told Chandra that they were testing the pickup driver for DUI. The policeman approached her to ask her why she stopped and why she was talking to Chandra. She said that she wanted to make sure that everyone was okay. He then asked her if she had seen the brake lights of the other vehicles ahead of Chandra, and she said that she did. She also told him that she had seen Chandra's brake lights come on.

The place where Chandra was employed at the time had her file any accident claims against their vehicles and equipment. Chandra sprang into action by getting the woman's name and phone number as a witness. Chandra also started taking pictures of her vehicle, the scene where it happened and the pickup that hit her. The woman then left the scene. Chandra was very thankful that this woman had stopped to help her!

The policeman told Chandra that she would get the police report to file with her insurance. The tow truck arrived to load Chandra's smashed, brand-new, leased Kia Sportage named "Penny Lincoln." Her grandchildren named it since it was copper in color, so it was the same color as a penny.

Chandra's head was spinning, and her neck hurt a little. She took some items out of Penny Lincoln, and the tow truck driver took over to load the car. Chandra climbed into the tow truck cab for a ride to the Holiday Station. She had called her boyfriend to pick her up there. Chandra also sent pictures of the accident to her children and told them she was okay. This was a bit of a curvy start to the weekend!

Chandra rested at her boyfriend's house most of the weekend. He drove her home on Sunday so she could go to her doctor on Monday to make sure that she didn't have any injuries besides being sore and shaken.

At her doctor's appointment, they found that she had whiplash. Chandra called the chiropractor to see if he could help with the whiplash. He wanted her to have an MRI to make sure there were no other injuries. She set up the appointment, and the MRI found nothing else. Chandra had several chiropractor appointments to help with the whiplash, and she also had daily exercises to do. Chandra's neck still makes a cracking noise when she turns her head a certain way.

Coworkers had been picking up Chandra to give her rides to work and home, but she knew this couldn't go on forever. She knew she needed a car even though she was not thrilled about driving for a while. She googled an AWD SUV with low mileage and discovered a 2015 Chevy Trax AWD with 15,000 miles within her budget. She purchased the vehicle and still has "Lucky Red Ruby," which was the name given by her grandson.

Chandra still has anxiety about driving in congested traffic, so she takes many back roads instead of busy roads.

She thought that living in a world with teleporting would be wonderful! In the blink of an eye, you could be at your destination!

CHAPTER 22

Chandra's life was going well! Her journey continued to be straight and smooth, but then the world stopped. On March 18, 2020, her place of employment was told that everyone needed to pack everything they needed to work from home as Covid 19 had become a pandemic. Places of employment were closed to the public since it was very contagious and, in some cases, deadly. The government was calling it "Safe at Home."

What a strange feeling she had being isolated in her own home to work without seeing other human beings.

Loneliness crept into her life again but thank goodness FaceTime and other social media kept her sane!

Small businesses were shut down, and large businesses stayed open, but people had to wear masks while running errands. Schools were doing online learning, so children were doing schoolwork at home while parents did their work online unless they were in the medical, construction, or other field where their work had to be done on-site.

The isolation of not seeing family or friends in person was very difficult for Chandra. She loved to socialize and go out dancing. Many weekend nights she listened to online concerts and danced alone in her living room. Many holidays were spent alone again, and this made her very heartbroken.

Chandra went into the office once a week to get the mail and take care of other paperwork that couldn't be done at home. Nobody else was in the office so she wasn't exposed to anyone. Chandra worked from home for six more weeks and then everyone was brought back to the office. They had to stay six feet away from each other and wear masks at all times.

Being back in the presence of other people and being able to converse and share experiences brought excitement back into her life!

On February 22, 2021, the students could return to school for in person learning. Chandra thought as most people did that it was such a strange time. Missing family gatherings, graduations, weddings, and other events.

The good things that Chandra thought came out of the pandemic were vaccines for Covid 19, people could work remotely, children spent more time with their family, and some people left the workforce to pursue their dreams and became self-employed. Covid 19 is still and will probably always be around.

CHAPTER 23

After being isolated during the pandemic, Chandra wanted to become more involved in her community. Chandra was invited by a friend to become a member of the Lions Club in her community. It is a great International Club! The motto is "We Serve." They sponsor many community events to raise money to donate back to the community. It is a great way to meet wonderful people also!

She was wearing her Lions vest one night at a Lions Burger Night in August 2021. A young woman at the bar asked her what Lions was all about, and she told her that they raise money to donate to community functions and help others in need.

The older gentleman sitting next to the young lady at the bar said, "I haven't seen you here before."

Chandra answered. "I am only here a few times monthly for Lions meetings and events.

He said, "I'm not here that often since I go to Florida from October to May. Then I return to my lake home for the summer months."

Chandra became very interested since her fourth dream was to be a snowbird and live in a warm, sunny place in the winter when she retired.

She asked him, "Where do you go?"

He explained to her about a 55+ mobile home park close to the beaches and on the Intracoastal. He told Chandra that some people rent out their mobile homes, so they exchanged numbers so Chandra could get more information from him when she retired.

When she retired, she contacted him to get more information, and he sent her the name of a lady from Canada who could possibly help her.

Chandra contacted the lady from Canada. She gave Chandra the name of a person from New York State who might be interested in renting his trailer.

For the last three years, Chandra and her boyfriend have been snowbirds in this wonderful, warm, sunny community!

They have met many good friends and gone on many adventures. Each year they are snowbirds, they plan on finding new places in the area to visit. There are many interesting places to explore!

Chandra's road to life is going straight and smooth right now. She worked hard all her life and now retirement holds new adventures! She has learned how to handle the curves when they come her way by perseverance, resilience, and probably some stubbornness. This is not the end for Chandra since she continues to grow as she wakes up daily to get behind the wheel and drive the road of life!

Hezzie Mae: All Things Beautiful

Hezzie Mae empowers and supports humans in telling their stories.

I am a trauma survivor whose life was forever changed when I penned and published my memoir. Hezzie Mae is a unique space for those with a story to tell, offering a unique blend of empathy from a survivor with the skills only a seasoned educator could bring.

How many of you have a story but haven't found the time or support to bring it to life?

www.HezzieMae.com

Heather N. Wilde is an indie publisher, illustrator & artist, speaker, writer, and trauma survivor. She is the author of *Tumbled: A Memoir or Perseverance, Personal Growth & Magical Transformation*, *Pig Tales and Popcorn: Patricia's Memoir*, and *Sell Your Book, Not Your Soul*. She watercolor-illustrated *Precious Child*, a timeless children's book. She speaks on accountability, personal growth, and recovering from trauma with the potential to lead an extraordinary life.

www.ingramcontent.com/pod-product-compliance
Lightning Source LLC
Jackson TN
JSHW071957100925
90830JS00017B/122